D1633267

JUNE FOURTH ELEGIES

念念六四

JUNE FOURTH ELEGIES

刘晓波
Liu Xiaobo

Translated from the Chinese by Jeffrey Yang

Foreword by His Holiness the Dalai Lama

CAPE POETRY

Published by Jonathan Cape 2012

2 4 6 8 10 9 7 5 3 1

Copyright © 2012 by Liu Xiaobo

Liu Xiaobo has asserted his right under the Copyright, Designs
and Patents Act 1988 to be identified as the author of this work

English Translation of the Author's Introduction and Poems, Notes, and Translator's Afterword
copyright © 2012 by Jeffrey Yang

Some of these translations first appeared in the following publications:

PEN America and the PEN American Center website, Melbourne PENQuarterly in Australia,
Index on Censorship in collaboration with the Writers in Prison Committee of English PEN,
I have no enemies (a pamphlet published for the Nobel Peace Prize Laureate exhibition at the
Nobel Peace Center), and the New York Times. Special thanks to Thomas Bredsdorff who
translated one poem for a broadside published in the Danish newspaper Politiken.

Audio recordings of some of these translations can be heard on the websites for the PEN
American Center, LYRIC Nation, Peace Talks Radio, and the PBS NewsHour Art Beat.

One poem was also read as part of a ballet performance by the principal dancers of the
Rambert Dance Company at the Royal Court Theatre in London for the annual
fundraising event for Human Rights Watch.

This book is sold subject to the condition that it shall not, by way of trade or otherwise, be lent,
resold, hired out, or otherwise circulated without the publisher's prior consent in any form
of binding or cover other than that in which it is published and without a similar condition,
including this condition, being imposed on the subsequent purchaser

First published in the United States in 2012 by Graywolf Press

First published in Great Britain in 2012 by
Jonathan Cape
Random House, 20 Vauxhall Bridge Road,
London SW1V 2SA

www.randomhouse.co.uk

Addresses for companies within The Random House Group Limited can be found at:
www.randomhouse.co.uk/offices.htm

The Random House Group Limited Reg. No. 954009

A CIP catalogue record for this book is available from the British Library

ISBN 9780224096812

The Random House Group Limited supports The Forest Stewardship Council (FSC®), the
leading international forest certification organisation. Our books carrying the FSC label are
printed on FSC® certified paper. FSC is the only forest certification scheme endorsed by
the leading environmental organisations, including Greenpeace. Our paper procurement
policy can be found at www.randomhouse.co.uk/environment

MIX
Paper from
responsible sources
FSC® C016897

Printed and bound in Great Britain by the MPG Books Group, Bodmin, Cornwall

*This book is dedicated to
the Tiananmen Mothers
and for those who can remember*

Contents

Foreword

As a firm believer in non-violence, freedom, and democratic values, I have supported the non-violent democracy movement in China from its beginning. One of the most encouraging and moving events in recent Chinese history was the democracy movement of 1989, when Chinese brothers and sisters demonstrated openly and peacefully their yearning for freedom, democracy, and human dignity. They embraced non-violence in a most impressive way, clearly reflecting the values their movement sought to assert.

The Chinese leadership's response to the peaceful demonstrations of 1989 was both inappropriate and unfortunate. Brute force, no matter how powerful, can never subdue the basic human desire for freedom, whether it is expressed by Chinese democrats and farmers or the people of Tibet.

In 2008, I was personally moved as well as encouraged when hundreds of Chinese intellectuals and concerned citizens inspired by Liu Xiaobo signed Charter 08, calling for democracy and freedom in China. I expressed my admiration for their courage and their goals in a public statement, two days after it was released. The international community also recognised Liu Xiaobo's valuable contribution in urging China to take steps toward political, legal, and constitutional reforms by supporting the award of the Nobel Peace Prize to him in 2010.

It is ironic that today, while the Chinese government is very concerned to be seen as a leading world power, many Chinese people from all walks of life continue to be deprived of their basic rights. In this collection of poems entitled *June Fourth Elegies,* Liu Xiaobo pays a moving tribute to the sacrifices made during the events in Tiananmen Square in 1989. Considering the writer himself remains imprisoned, this book serves as a powerful reminder of his courage and determination and his great-hearted concern for the welfare of his fellow countrymen and women.

His Holiness the Fourteenth Dalai Lama, Tenzin Gyatso

3 September, 2011

Author's Introduction

From the Tremors of a Tomb

31 December, 1999, the eve of a new millennium. Everyone in Beijing was busy preparing their festive celebrations. A friend phoned from the street, crying out in agony that the markets were so packed with people disaster was imminent. Another friend phoned inviting me and my wife, Liu Xia, over for drinks and some card playing, but we had accepted an earlier invitation a while back and were going to visit two Renmin University professors, Ding Zilin and Jiang Peikun. My wife and I must have unconsciously wanted to offer the eve of the new millennium to the departed souls of June Fourth.

With their family of three – the two teachers Ding and Jiang, and their daughter – we ate a simple dinner. After chatting for a while and catching up, the mood quickly turned serious. Each of us sitting there tried to think of something lighthearted to talk about, and yet, between our shared memories and adverse circumstances, we really couldn't think of anything to say that would make us laugh out loud or at least amuse us for a moment of relief. Teacher Ding repeatedly exhorted me to please take good care of Liu Xia from now on. I knew this was really his sincere concern for my own welfare – one human being's concern for another. In the past decade Teacher Ding has been consumed with assisting families who had lost loved ones during June Fourth, helping them with their daily subsistence, bearing those innocent departed souls to their surviving family; for it wasn't just the sorrow of losing a loved one, but more significantly it was a totalitarian state's brutal persecution and conscienceless indifference toward society that have created a collective amnesia. Teacher Ding deeply empathises with the loved ones of our society's dissenters who must carry on in intense anguish.

When it was time to leave, Ding and Jiang gave us the written record of their long-suffering tribulations, *Seeking Justice for the Witnessed Massacre*, which contained a list of 155 casualties of June Fourth along with testimonies of survivors, and then exhorted me again to please, please look after Liu Xia.

On the road home, my wife and I remained silent. As we neared our place we quickly discovered that our street had been blocked off, vehicles unable to pass. A policeman, face taut and directing cars with brusque gestures, unexpectedly enlightened me: 'Eh, there's another tire-the-people-drain-the-treasury farce tonight at the altar of the newly built China Millennium Monument, and coincidentally this road leads straight there, no more than a two kilometer stretch.'

In China, the twentieth century didn't end on 31 December, 1999, but rather on 1 October, on the occasion of the fiftieth anniversary of the ruling Communist Party. With corruption spreading thick, popular grievances boiling over, what is the morality in wasting one hundred billion yuan to stage a huge tire-the-people-drain-the-treasury celebration? It's hard to imagine how much Chinese citizens have suffered these past fifty years, and yet has anyone in power even once said to the populace, 'I'm sorry.' Besides spreading lies to the public while pounding one's own drum, this grand festivity for the fiftieth anniversary is merely a celebration of extravagance, a cult of personality, disguising the government's fear and anxiety with the pretence of prosperity. China – whose experiences of suffering and national absurdities are rare in the world – till today has yet to undergo a process of wakening and repentance, but instead intensifies its flashy bubble of prosperity coupled with a vain servility. Can we still possibly save ourselves?

As the twenty-first century began, those in power insisted on imitating the Chinese emperors of the past and staged a single performance at the sacrificial altar. Beijing has served as the site for many ancient dynastic capitals – relics and ruins are everywhere – so it's especially easy for people to associatively think of an autocratic monarchy. In this place long ago emperors presided over ritual offerings to Heaven at the Temple of Earth and the Temple of Heaven, though for the purpose of ushering in the twenty-first century, to build another 'Temple of the Chinese Century', another tire-the-people-drain-the-treasury (while the General Secretary craves greatness as Premier Engineer) just to satisfy the vanity of the potentates, and then with work not completed yet rush to open it to the public (nearly half a year had passed and the Millennium Monument was still a closed construction site) – even the taxi drivers saw it as a kind of monarchical, ritual demonstration of supreme imperial power.

In the face of a nation that shamelessly assails the very marrow of our bones, memory is but a pale grey field. To use 'amnesia', 'blasphemous spleen', 'soullessness', and other such descriptive phrases I feel is so much wasted praise and a great irreverence to those forsaken departed souls. Sifting through the storehouse of my vocabulary, I'm unable to find a fitting word and have no alternative but to use Lu Xun's sardonic 'national profanity' to loudly shout, 'MOTHERFUCKER!'

2

Once home, before even taking a sip of water and with an impatience too burning to wait, I flipped open *Seeking Justice for the Witnessed Massacre*; as I read the first page my eyes began to blur with tears. I read some aloud to Liu Xia, unable to finish the briefest passage before breaking into sobs, and though I cannot remember now how many times I broke off, each broken moment of silence was like death's stillness: one could hear the cries of injustice from those departed souls buried beneath the earth, their cries so faint, so helpless, so heart-lung-rending. Teachers, we give you our heartfelt thanks for allowing such an extraordinary means of spending that New Year's Eve of the new millennium while so many others put on conventional ritualistic, cultural airs. For as a majestic, resplendent ceremony beyond compare was taking place not far from our home, the night and the departed souls became intertwined, consoling our hearts so that we felt at peace. My wife and I both agreed that this was what infused that New Year's Eve with such a profound significance. Now, as I sit at my computer writing this memorial for June Fourth, my ears can still hear the soundless cries of those dead souls.

Eleven years have passed – between the executioners and the survivors what have we really done for the aggrieved ghosts of the innocents? Within the last nine months Communist Party authorities have perpetrated some of the most contemptible actions: first, detaining the activist Lu Wenhe in Shanghai to block overseas humanitarian donations to families of those killed on 4 June; then in Beijing intercepting two white-haired mothers to prevent them from meeting. One mother had been seeking justice for her seventeen-year-old son who was shot and killed during martial law. After the tragedy, she was summoned by the CCP police, spied on, followed, put under house arrest, among other such harassments – ten years like a day hurrying for the grave, by way of a mother's tenacious love, an intellectual's unrelenting search for knowledge that exposed lies and interrogated a cold-blooded society in order to appease both the departed souls buried beneath the earth and the loved ones left upon the earth, dispelling the inner fears of those loved ones and gradually consolidating community strength in facing a dictatorship's abuses of power. The other mother had crossed the ocean with her son to once more pay respects at her husband's grave in a faraway land, while also hoping to meet Madame Ding Zilin to convey her protestations against the massacre, her humanitarian concerns toward the families of the killed, and her admiration of Professor Ding. Her husband was once close to the Communist Party during one of its most troubled periods, and as an American journalist he publicised overwhelming moral support for the secession of the Yanan, Shanbei regime. But Madame Snow never thought the CCP was such a cynical political party – yesterday: sweet-talking her with honey words, praising Mr Snow for his enormous dedication to the Chinese Revolution, that he was a steadfast old pal of the Party and Madame Snow had come to sweep his grave personally accompanied by Zhou Enlai; and today: skinning aside any appearance of face, staring at each other with glowering eyes, tapping phones and sending out numerous policemen to harass her, and of course don't speak of reputation, morality, friendship. As the proposed appeals of these two mothers were quite simple and direct, so much so that they didn't even need to meet to discuss them, Madame Snow decided to write a personal letter to Premier Zhu Rongji. But the reply to these two white-haired mothers was yet more police officers cutting them off from the rest of the world.

With a government like this, what about the populace? In an autocratic power structure replete with the little comforts bribes concede, the majority of people remain silent, numbed, soaked in the affected unconventionality of Yu Qiuyu's bitter journey through culture and his *Yongzheng Dynasty*'s flattering self-righteous praise song. Yu's book transforms an escape from reality into a resentment of tradition, or as Zhu Da Ke put it, 'Turns a lost civilisation into the condom of culture, the lipstick of culture', evoking a kind of safe faddism and painful cultural posturing. Or consider what's been called 'the most inquisitive, most energetic, most stimulating' of the new generation of Chinese writers in authentic Hong Kong-Taiwan Mandarin, and read the fully bared sex, crime, drugs, and loads of name-brand fashion of *Shanghai Baby* and *Candy*, what in the West has long been old hat – cliché New York, cliché Paris, cliché decadent taste – and wholly lacking in any 'Chinese characteristics'. Or compare Wang Shuo's 'hooligan' style to Liu Sola's typical hippieness. The new generation rarely directs their blasphemous rebelliousness toward totalitarian ideology, and is mostly concerned with reveling in the ephemeral pleasures of the present – their self-absorption and self-pity borderline pathological as they intentionally plunge into the debauchery of love-whoever-wherever, dwelling on the ephemeral feelings and minor matters of an individual's superficial sufferings that truly deserve the little comforts of the times, as if they're living an obscene, desolate, drunken dream between life and death. They face the ruthless realities of a totalitarian system with extreme world-wise unction – yesterday: indignant denouncements before the US embassy in China; today: standing in the long visa-application line to study abroad in the US. In this age of illusions, they've mastered the astonishing craftiness of a trickster and know when and in what situation to approach which person with keen blade raised or an offering of roses. They've matured without experiencing innocence; they've given up without experiencing the pursuit.

If one says that our parents' generation as well as our generation have been brainwashed by both Communist class struggle and Buddhist asceticism, we will have lost the memories and visions of a glorious humanity; and yet this new generation has been brainwashed by the materialism and hedonism of the Communist Party: they have no memory of the past sufferings of the Chinese people. Seventy years ago, totalitarian rule in the Soviet Union left the population with the proper noun, 'Gulag'; fascist rule during the Second World War also left the world with another proper noun, 'Auschwitz'. And us? A frightening emptiness: only the artificiality of cheap high-rise towers, not a trace of the grave's ever blooming flowers.

But still, compared to a survivor like myself, a June Fourth celebrity like myself, a self-proclaimed cultural elitist like myself, what have we done for those departed souls? My good friend, the Sichuan poet Liao Yiwu, after the bloody events of 4/6 wrote two long poems, 'Massacre' and 'Requiem', for which he was accused as the chief instigator of the 'crime to incite counter-revolutionary propaganda' and sentenced to four years in prison. It wasn't until the end of 1999 that I heard him read 'Massacre' at a friend's place, or rather recite not read, or not recite – nor shout nor roar – but a rare, solemn display of the physicality of words that required the activation of the body's whole force and strength to complete (a hollowing of the flesh and extracting of the bones). In the final section of the poem, I thought I could hear a tortuous, self-questioning ripping noise from his vocal cords saying, *Who are the survivors? The survivors are all sons of bitches!* – though I feel our company of survivors are even inferior to motherfucking sons of bitches! Dogs retain their dog-nature but do we as humans still retain our humanity?! Those self-professed intellectuals with so-called intuitive knowledge, why ask them to boldly step forward in the massacre's terrifying aftermath, rank with blood, so as to show that one's own humanity barely exists, for we are told that even during the Holocaust few people dared to go into the streets to care for the dead and wounded. And as of the turn of this century no one's yet written our 'In Memory of the Noble Miss Liu Hezhen'. It's apparent that Lu Xun possessed all the qualifications to deride the many assorted intellectuals throughout Chinese history. After all, one flash of the venomous glare from Lu Xun's eyes revealed that China has never had an independent intelligentsia. At the beginning of the last century, Chinese watched Japanese kill Chinese citizens with a wooden face and foolish smile as if observing the expressions of a guest; as the century closed, the Chinese faced the horrifying genocide carried out by totalitarian states with a cowardly stance of cold detachment and obliviousness. One hundred years of suffering and suddenly nothing's changed: 'Time forever sails on: the metropolis as of yesteryear calm and peaceful – for in China, a limited number of lives lost counts for nothing. At most, it merely gives thoughtless idlers something to talk about after a meal, or provides thinking idlers seeds for gossip.' Truly life counts for nothing into the new century, yesteryear's darkness unchanged even if there is the faintest glimmer of light, which isn't 'the courage of the true brave warrior' who 'dares to face the wretchedness of life, dares to witness spilled blood', but rather the greed of parasites, the gleam from a coward's eyes.

3

Teachers Ding and Jiang's cause arose from the renouncement of their solitary sorrow: these passing years they've both cared for and encouraged each and every person they've come across who happened to have shared their fate. Such a humble, honest, flesh-and-blood just cause permeating the earth with warmth and kindness is far from any 'looking down upon all living creatures from on high preaching trying to pass as giving'. As they both travelled around the country looking for family traces of those lost on 4 June, I could still see the little that remained of real intuitive knowledge, of love's tenacity. This, I believe, is the only living memory left of 4/6 – and the most worthy and just of causes. If all the other survivors were like them and made even the smallest effort for those innocent dead souls, the executioners could never have continued to be so unscrupulous after killing so many people – the tomb of June Fourth would never have become so forsaken.

In *Seeking Justice for the Witnessed Massacre*, the most heart-and-lung rending thing for my wife was that those whose lives were so casually extinguished by the bloodlusters in power weren't part of any privileged group but were ordinary civilians content with their simple desires and common needs. These were people who never tried to block any military vehicles, never even tried to see the excitement, but while chatting in their courtyard at home were suddenly killed by a stray bullet, or while walking on the street by chance crossed paths with martial-law-enforcing officers, or randomly chased down and killed by soldiers with red-death in their eyes. But certain self-serving, elitist philistines were also survivors of the slaughterer's knife – even if they had once been forced into exile overseas, they were still arrested and imprisoned in this country, and thus muddled into a small or large reputation, received a small or large measure of solicitude. Recently, the Communist regime was granted Permanent Normal Trade Relations (PNTR) with the US, bringing forward the early release of 4/6 political prisoner Chen Lantao. After hearing about the massacre, this young man from Qingdao had given only one public speech in protest and was handed a severe eighteen-year sentence, while the maximum prison sentence for those famous arrested '4/6 black hands' in Beijing was thirteen years – and each of these individuals received early release. From the beginning of June 1989, I've been imprisoned three times and released three times, though if you add up the total amount of time I've lost it comes to about six years. In the whole of China, in numerous places outside of Beijing, those given harsh thirteen-year sentences are like the unknown, non-celebrity Chen Lantao, and many are still in prison cells.

What, then, is the real truth of June Fourth's history? Why do college students and the intellectual elite attach such great importance to the '89 Movement, despite the fact that when the tragedy happened those who were killed were mainly common citizens, and those who were arrested and severely sentenced were also mainly common citizens? Why are the silenced nobodies who paid the highest price with their lives powerless to narrate history, but those privileged elite seen as fortunate survivors have the authority to chatter on and on without rest? Why after June Fourth is the blood of common citizens still used to nourish opportunists of all stripes who shamelessly presume that the so-called 'democracy movement' is actually a vanity fair? What is suffering and sacrifice? What is life and the price of blood? In this land of ours, the distribution of happiness has long been as divided as heaven and earth. Could it be then that suffering is a kind of natural resource, that those who suffer equally or by degrees, unequally, are thus destined to be as divided as heaven and earth?

To this day in China, we haven't been able to overcome the cold-blooded self-interests of totalitarianism, but at the very least we could exercise self-discipline, hold fast to the crux of humanity in valuing freedom and the countless individuals who replenish life's natural resources of morality and justice: the only natural resources we have in resisting tyranny. The hanging medals of suffering that fill the chests of the elite mean nothing, and even signify a negation of suffering. Can we not expend a little fraternal love and cultivate a yearning for equality and a moral society by serving those who have suffered deeply as they strived for the justice that originally should have belonged to them? Deep in the stillness of the night, staring into our very soul, do we still truly feel in our innermost being the pain and moral necessity of guilt? If so, then for the moment a grain of good still lingers in the disaster; if not, then there's nothing left. Eleven years have passed and the blood of June Fourth – save for what goes into the steamed human-blood buns that are fed to the 'heroic men of the passing wind and clouds' here or abroad – has scarcely allowed our callous, obscene nation to attain even a crumb of progress. Suffering is a natural resource: an individual, or nation, who refuses to forget could transform this natural resource into soul-ascending wealth. But in China, suffering has always been only a fishing-for-medals-and-straw natural resource, and very rarely transforms into wealth. So let us recognise our shame and guilt; let us ache with self-reflection; let us eradicate the repetition of suffering and resist anger; let us learn to concretely tend to the suffering of an individual, of our common citizens, with equality; let us learn how to live life with honour and dignity and a wealth of humanity.

4

These past ten years, I've often been plagued by a guilty conscience. When I was in Qincheng Prison I betrayed the blood of the departed souls by writing a confession. After I was released, I still had a somewhat notorious reputation and received an excessive amount of attention. But the ordinary victims, the nameless who to this day are still in jail – what have they received? Whenever I think about this, I can't bear to gaze into the depths of my soul – there are too many weaknesses to face, too much selfishness, too many shameless lies. For too long now we've leaned upon the blade of the bayonet's lies, shamelessness, selfishness, weaknesses, so that we've wholly lost both memory and time – life numbed, unceasing and interminable, from zero begins to zero it ends: what qualifications can we claim for our mighty nation? None with the least merit. And what remains for us? Across this land even the deserts are at fault. The deserts with their vast nothingness and desolation – is this what's left for us? I, too, eat steamed human-blood buns: at the most I form decorative ornaments against an anti-humanist system – caught then released, released then caught – and do not know when this game will ever end, nor know if I've actually done anything for the departed souls, to be able to let myself recollect with a clear heart and conscience.

I long to use resistance and imprisonment as atonement, to try to realise my idealistic convictions with integrity, but this creates deep, painful wounds for my family. In truth, imprisonment for me, for activists working against an authoritarian system, is nothing to flaunt – it's a necessary honour living at the mercy of an inhuman regime, where there's little choice for the individual but resistance. Inasmuch as resistance is a choice, imprisonment is simply a part of this choice: the inevitable vocation of traitors of a totalitarian state, like a peasant must take to the fields, or as a student must read books. Inasmuch as resistance is a choice to descend into hell, one mustn't complain about the darkness; as far as I think there's an indestructible wall up ahead, I still must exert the strength to smash into it – and the wound in my head that flows with blood is self-inflicted: one cannot resent anyone cannot blame anyone, but must bear the wound alone. Who was it who let you deliberately fly like a moth into the flame, rather than circle around?

As I toasted the elders of the autocracy, and my unwavering stance – with a righteousness inspiring reverence – won me the brave epithet of 'democracy activist' with an awareness that this was a moment of consummate achievement and virtue – precisely then the slow inner torment of my close, extended family began. Each day I'm rarely concerned with the actual people who live around me, but am usually only concerned with sublime abstractions: justice, human rights, freedom. I use my family for my day's security as I gaze with troubled heart and trembling flesh upon the everyday failings of the world. During a three-year prison sentence, my wife made thirty-eight trips from Beijing to Dalian to see me, and eighteen of these trips she couldn't even bear to actually face me and quickly dropped some things off and hurried back alone. Trapped in an icy loneliness, unable to preserve the slightest amount of privacy while being followed and spied on, she tirelessly waited tirelessly struggled, with a hair-turning-white-overnight perseverance. I'm punished by the dictatorship in the form of a prison; I punish my family by creating a formless prison around their hearts.

This is a particular kind of totalitarian cruelty where the bloodshed remains unseen – and in China it is especially cruel and severe. From the time agrarian reform was initiated in the 1950s ('suppress counter-revolutionaries', 'ideological remoulding', the Three-Anti/Five-Anti Campaigns, the Gao-Rao Anti-party Group, the Hu Feng Anti-party Group, 'purge counter-revolutionaries', 'socialist transformation of industry and commerce', the Anti-Rightest Movement) to the 1960s and 1970s (the Four Cleanups Movement, the Socialist Education Movement, the Cultural Revolution, 'criticise the rightist deviationist wind of reversing verdicts', the April Fifth Movement) then through the 1980s and 1990s (the Anti-Spiritual Pollution Campaign, the

Anti-Liberalisation Campaign, the June Fourth Movement, 'suppress the Democratic Party and all other political dissidents', 'crack down on the Falun Gong and all non-governmental organisations'), fifty years have passed: China grows in enormity with a population of 1.9 billion and yet it's nearly impossible to find a whole family intact; man and wife divided; father and son turned enemies; friends betray each other; a dissident tries to implicate a group of innocents; an individual's imprisoned for holding different political views – among family and friends we all must bear unlawful harassment from the police.

While across this stretch of earth, so many innocent victims are condemned and even derided behind the so-called 'selflessness' of career politicians. For their own power, reputation, status, and so-called 'perfection of character' – in order to receive the adoration of a god – they treat people as their personal stepping-stones; even those closest to them can only serve the authorities' absolute perfection and sacrifice everything for nothing. China's ancient political wisdom and political character, too, was one of 'self-perfection to achieve selflessness', and was marked by a cold-bloodedness that lacked a shred of humanity or human happiness – from the mythical Yu the Great trying to tame the floods for thirteen years and *passing his home three times and not entering once to see his family* to Mao Zedong's wife who died in prison – such has been consecrated as a paragon of political character. The victors in particular among them never say to those they've victimised (including their own family), 'I'm sorry'; their hearts ever at peace without any anguish (at most they assume the *appearance* of a guilty conscience and remorse). Instead, they transform these victims into saintly, godly capital for themselves to flaunt about society – upon their own fake faces they paste another layer of gold.

If the excessive blood-soaked policies of the totalitarian state didn't exist, a politician would have no need to let others sacrifice so much; and family, in particular, pay the highest price of the sacrificed. Often when I think about the road of resistance I've chosen, scattered with the sacrifices my family's been forced to make, it's almost unbearable. During these recurring moments I truly resent myself, to the point that I feel I am indeed a most repugnant cause.

Long before June Fourth, I had been digging plots of unfilial piety and national nihilism in the ancestral graveyard; yet what nation do I face – 'motherland': this large, empty word has always retained a suspicious posturing, and especially for us here patriotism is a villain's last refuge. I've never been one to ask about a person's race or ethnic background, but instead ask about the place where this person became one of many unique individuals, if life there upholds dignity, civil rights, freedom, love, beauty. Long ago I once made an excessive statement about 'three hundred years of colonisation'; today, I lean toward 'comprehensive westernisation', in the sense of 'westernisation' meaning humanisation: to treat people equally as human beings. For in China, past and present, the government has never treated its citizens as human beings, to the extent that the Chinese people must experience the servitude of Wang Shuo's *Please Don't Call Me Human* to know how to live. And China's so-called intelligentsia is, for the most part, the dictator's conspirator and accomplice. Some have called me conceited, and yet I cannot deny the awe and humility I feel deep within my soul. In the presence of Christ's sacrifice, in the presence of Kafka's desperation, in the presence of the true backbone of Lu Xun's *courage to embrace the corpses of dissenters with bitter tears*, in the presence of Kant's wisdom, in the presence of Daoist metaphysician Jin Yuelin's pure love for Lin Huiyin, I'm always the smallest of humans.

In 1988 Jiang Peikun was on my doctoral defence committee, and so one could say that on our visit to his home that New Year's Eve, being able to call him and his wife my teachers was determined by chance and proper etiquette; after reading their witnessed account of the dead, however . . . *Ding Zilin, Jiang Peikun, you are two teachers who have my deepest admiration – not only for your rigorous intellect, but more so for your integrity. My two teachers – and the departed souls buried beneath the earth – please accept a student's reverence from one unworthy to be your student: with the awe and humility from the tremor of a soul.*

The anniversary of June Fourth is almost here again – my wife and I are most grateful for that eve of the millennium, which has been engraved in our memories for the rest of our lives. Of course that night wasn't extraordinarily significant *for* us, being just one night among countless nights, and yet possessed by the bitter grief of the tomb it continues to confront the memory of the departed spirits. The living should really shut their mouths and let the graves speak; let the dead souls teach the living what it means to live, what it means to die, what it means to be dead but still alive.

LIU XIAOBO
At home in Beijing, 14/5/2000

念念六四

June Fourth Elegies

1990年6月于秦城监狱

体验死亡
——"六·四"一周年祭

Experiencing Death

Qincheng Prison, June 1990
First anniversary offering for 4/6

一

纪念碑一阵阵抽泣
大理石的纹路浸透血迹
信念和青春扑倒在
坦克履带的铁锈下
东方古老的故事
突然新鲜欲滴

浩荡的人流渐渐消失
犹如一条慢慢干枯的河
两岸的风景化作石头
所有的喉咙被恐惧窒息
所有的颤抖随硝烟散去
只有刽子手的钢盔
闪闪发光

1

Monument waves of weeping
marble grain fused with blood-stained veins
Belief and youth beaten beneath
a tank's rust-chained treads
Ancient story of the East
leaks out new hope unexpectedly

The glorious crowds have little by little disappeared
like a river that slowly, steadily dries away
landscape on both shores transformed to stone
Every throat has been strangled by fear, every
trembling has traced the dissipated niter smoke
Only the executioner's steel
helmet glints, luminous glints

二

我不再认识旗帜
旗帜象还不懂事的孩子
扑在妈妈尸体上
哭喊着回家
我再不能分辨白昼和黑夜
时间被枪声惊呆
如同失去记忆的植物人
枪口顶住我的后腰
我丢掉了身份证和护照

在刺刀挑起的黎明中
那个曾经熟悉的世界
找不到一捧泥土
掩埋自己

赤裸的心
与钢铁碰撞
没有水没有绿的大地
一任阳光蹂躏

2

I cannot recognise the flag anymore
The flag like an unknowing child
who's flung upon Mother's corpse
returns home weeping
I cannot tell day from night anymore
Time has been petrified by gunshots
like a paralytic without memory
Gun's muzzle presses into my back
I've lost my passport and identity card

In the bayonet-inflamed dawn
that once familiar world
cannot find a handful of dirt
to bury itself in

Naked red heart
collides with iron and steel
Earth without water without greenness
ravaged by sunlight

三

他们等呀等
等待时间编出精致的谎言
等待变成野兽的时刻
直等到
手指变成利爪
眼睛变成枪口
双脚变成履带
空气变成命令
来了
终于来了
那个等了五千年的命令

开枪——杀人
杀人——开枪
和平请愿与手无寸铁
拄拐的白发与扯着衣襟的小手
决不能说服刽子手
眼睛烧红了
枪筒打红了
双手染红了
一粒子弹
一股浑浊的宣泄
一次犯罪
一种英雄的壮举

多么轻松
死亡如此降临
多么容易
兽欲得到满足
年轻的士兵
也许刚刚穿上军装
还没有经历过
被姑娘亲吻的醉意

3

They wait and wait
wait for time to invent an exquisite lie
wait for the transformation of the bestial hour
Indeed, wait until
fingers transform to sharpened claws
eyes transform to a gun's mouth
feet transform to chained treads
air transforms to a command
It arrives
at last it arrives
the five-thousand-year awaited command

Open fire – kill people
kill people – open fire
Peaceful petition, hands unarmed
an old man's cane, a child's torn jacket
The executioner will never be swayed
Eyes burnt to red
Gun-barrels shot to red
Hands dyed red
A bullet
A mud-thick secret spills out
A crime
A kind of heroic feat

How relaxing
death's arrival
How easy
bestial desires are satisfied
Young soldiers
recently clothed in uniform
still haven't felt
the intoxication of a girl's kiss

却在刹那间
体验到嗜血的快感
用杀人开始了他们的青春

他们
看不见浸透连衣裙的血
听不见挣扎着的尖叫
钢盔的坚硬感觉不到生命的脆弱
他们不知道
一个昏庸的老人
正在把古老的京城
变成又一处奥斯维辛

残忍与罪恶拔地而起
象金字塔一样辉煌
而生命崩溃如深渊
听不到一丝回响
屠杀雕刻出一个民族的传统
岁月悠悠，如废弃的语言
做最后的诀别

but now in an instant
experience the bloodthirsty pleasure
of murder, their youth's beginnings

They who
cannot see the blood-soaked dress
cannot hear the struggle's scream
through steel helmets cannot perceive life's fragility
They aren't aware
of the fatuous old man
transforming the ancient capital
into another zone of Auschwitz

Brutality, iniquity rise up from the earth
like the splendour of a pyramid
while life crumbles into the abyss
where even the faintest echo cannot be heard
The massacre has engraved a nation's tradition
years, months as remote as an abandoned language
that enacts a final farewell

四

我本想在阳光下
加入殉道者的行列
用仅存的一根骨头
支撑起虔诚的信仰
但，天空并不会
为牺牲者镀上金黄
一群饱食死尸的狼
在正午的温暖中
喜气洋洋

遥远地
我把生命放逐到
一个没有太阳的地方
逃出耶稣生日的纪元
我不敢正视十字架上的目光
从一支烟到一小堆灰烬
我被烈士的酒灌醉
以为这个春天将繁花似锦

深夜、空旷的马路
我骑着自行车回家
我停在烟摊前
自行车被跟踪的车辆撞倒
几个大汉拦路抢劫
我被戴上手铐蒙住眼睛堵住嘴巴
扔进不知驶向何方的囚车

瞬间的颤抖过后
蓦然醒悟：我还活着
在中央电视台的 新闻联播中
我的名字变成被"抓住的黑手"
而 无名者的白骨
立在遗忘里

4

I had imagined being there beneath sunlight
with the procession of martyrs
using just the one thin bone
to uphold a true conviction
And yet, the heavenly void
will not plate the sacrificed in gold
A pack of wolves well-fed full of corpses
celebrate in the warm noon air
aflood with joy

Faraway place
I've exiled my life to
this place without sun
to flee the era of Christ's birth
I cannot face the blinding vision on the cross
From a wisp of smoke to a little heap of ash
I've drained the drink of the martyrs, sense spring's
about to break into the brocade-brilliance of myriad flowers

Deep in the night, empty road
I'm biking home
I stop at a cigarette stand
A car follows me, crashes over my bicycle
some enormous brutes seize me
I'm handcuffed eyes covered mouth gagged
thrown into a prison van heading nowhere

A blink, a trembling instant passes
to a flash of awareness: I'm still alive
On Central Television News
my name's changed to 'arrested black-hand'
though those nameless white bones of the dead
still stand in the forgetting

我被自编的谎言高高擎起
逢人便讲我体验过死亡
仿佛"黑手"就是一枚英雄勋章

尽管我知道
死是神秘的未知
活着，便无法体验死亡
而死了
就再不能体验死亡
但
我仍在死中飞翔
沉沦地飞翔
无数个铁窗后的夜晚
和星光下的坟墓
被我的噩梦出卖

除了谎言
我一无所有

I'm lifted up high by the self-invented lie
tell everyone how I've experienced death
so that 'black-hand' becomes a hero's medal of honour

Even if I know
death's a mysterious unknown
being alive, there's no way to experience death
and once dead
cannot experience death again
yet I'm still
hovering within death
a hovering in drowning
Countless nights behind iron-barred windows
and the graves beneath starlight
have exposed my nightmares

Besides a lie
I own nothing

1991年6月1日深夜于北京

给十七岁
——"六·四"二周年祭

For 17

Beijing, deep in the night, 1/6/1991
Second anniversary offering for 4/6

题记：你不听父母的劝阻，从家中厕所的小窗跳出；你擎着旗帜倒下时，仅十七岁。我却活下来，已经三十六岁。面对你的亡灵，活下来就是犯罪，给你写诗更是一种耻辱。活人必须闭嘴，听坟墓诉说。给你写诗，我不配。你的十七岁超越所有的语言和人工的造物.

我活着
还有个不大不小的臭名
我没有勇气和资格
捧着一束鲜花或一首诗
走到十七岁的微笑前

我知道
十七岁没有任何抱怨

十七岁的年龄告诉我
生命朴素无华
如同一望无际的沙漠
不需要树不需要水
不需要花的点缀
就能承受太阳的肆虐

十七岁倒在道路上
道路从此消失
泥土中长眠的十七岁
象书一样安详
十七岁来到世界上
什么也不依恋
除了洁白无暇的年龄

Dedication: At home, you didn't listen to the protests of mother or father and escaped through the small bathroom window; then the flag you raised collapsed, age 17. I'm still alive, already 36. Now, facing your departed spirit, being alive is a crime, writing you a poem a further disgrace. The living should really shut their mouths and listen to the graves speak. Writing you a poem I'm not worthy of. Your 17th year transcends all speech and man-made structures.

I'm still alive
with a name of some disrepute
I possess neither courage nor qualifications
holding a bouquet of flowers or a poem
walking toward the smile of 17

I know
17 bears no bitterness

17 tells me
life's simple without extravagance
as if gazing across a boundless desert
no need for trees no need for water
no need for the adornments of flowers
simply endure the tyranny of the sun

17 collapses on the path
the path disappears
17's long sleep underground
is as serene as a book
17 comes into the world
and is attached to nothing
save the pure white innocence of the age

十七岁停止呼吸时
奇迹般地没有绝望
子弹射穿了山脉
痉挛逼疯了海水
当所有的花，只有
一种颜色的时刻
十七岁没有绝望
不会绝望
十七岁把未完成的爱
交给满头白发的母亲

那位曾经把十七岁
反锁在家中的母亲
那位在五星红旗下
割断了家族的
高贵血缘的母亲
被你临终的眼神唤醒
她带着十七岁的遗嘱
走遍所有的坟墓
每一次她就要倒下时
十七岁都会用亡灵的气息
把她扶住
送她上路

超越了年龄
超越了死亡
十七岁
已经永恒

17 stops to breathe
and miraculously doesn't despair
A bullet's fired, crosses a mountain pass
churns the sea into madness
among the many flowers, there's only
a kind of colourful transience
17 doesn't despair
will not despair
17 takes love unfulfilled
and gives it to the white-haired mother

The mother who kept your 17th year
locked in the safety of home
The mother who beneath the red
five-starred flag, cut off from the dignity
of family blood-ties, awakened
the dying spirit in your eyes
She carries the will and testament of your 17th year
wanders among the graves
Whenever she's about to collapse
17 uses the breath of its departed spirit
to brace her
and show her the path

Age transcended
Death transcended
17th year as ever-
lasting

1992年6月6日于北京

窒息的广场
——"六·四"三周年祭

Suffocating City Square

Beijing, 6/6/1992
Third anniversary offering for 4/6

这个全世界最大的广场
挤满人群和呐喊
只是一瞬间
水银泻地般的奔逃
除了恐惧
就是空旷
殉道者的苍白中
钢盔与晨光共舞
被上帝审判的人
正透过某个窗口
欣赏着黎明之杯中
盛满的紫黑色液体

有勇气穿过广场的男人
也能徒步穿过太阳系
灰烬一旦燃烧
变成温暖的词
青涩的果实
在死亡中成熟
献给
不需要玫瑰的女人
她的嗓音照亮地狱
面对横冲过来的坦克
站着不动
挥舞柔软的手臂
如同一柄阴雨天的红伞

她倒下的一瞬间
四周一片空旷
是谁顺手丢下的废纸
落在她高耸的前胸
又被一阵风吹起
遮住那双修长的手臂
就算她从来没有读过《圣经》
也不该被上帝遗弃在

This city square the largest in the world
filled to the brink with crowds and cheers
in a blink liquid
mercury flash of fleeing
Now only fear
and an empty expanse remain
Against the ash-white pallor of the martyrs
dawn light dances on steel helmets
Those whom God judges
pass through certain windows
admire daybreak in a cup
that overflows with a bruise-coloured liquid

The courage that infuses the man in the city square
infuses the solar system with each stride
Embers burn to daybreak
become the dim warmth of a word
bitter green fruit
ripening in death
A dedication to
the woman who needs no rose
her voice lights up the inferno
facing the vicious roar of a tank
standing unmoving
waving a weakened arm as if
opening a red umbrella on a grey rainy day

In a blink she collapses
empty expanse in four directions
Whose carelessly tossed paper scraps
fall onto her lifted chest
rise up again with a gust of wind
shroud a slender pair of arms
Even if she's never read the Holy Scriptures
God shouldn't abandon her to

堆起垃圾的 路边
在小伙子的梦中
飘飞的长发
也不该让血污粘住

如果是另一个春天
她与男友手拉手
走在这个广场
她也许不会为
偶尔踩死的一只虫子
惊叹
此刻，她失血的双唇
惊呆了地下的蛀虫
它们犹豫地伸出夹子
抓到的只是血腥

这个被死亡掏空的广场
为了一种绝对的权力
窒息了所有生命
这个被死亡塑造的姑娘
为了一行纯粹的诗
放弃了所有文字

the heaps of garbage along the road
wisps of long hair float into
a boy's dream, shouldn't
allow this bloodbath-fastness

If it was a different spring
she would walk across this city square
hand in hand with her boyfriend
She wouldn't have become
a random insect crushed underfoot
Marvel
at this moment, her bloodless lips
the stunned moth-grubs underground
they hesitantly stretch out their pincers
but only grasp the stench of blood

This death-hollowed city square
for the sake of absolute power
suffocates all life
This death-cast girl
has become a line of pure poetry
that surrenders all ideograms

1993年5月31日于北京某酒吧

一颗烟独自燃烧
——"六·四"四周年祭

A Lone Cigarette Burns

A bar in Beijing, 31/5/1993
Fourth anniversary offering for 4/6

一颗独自燃烧的烟
咖啡
冰淇淋
威士忌中清凉的冰块
几个老外向我提问
那个春天的事情
我的回答有股
大饭店的洗手间和
公共厕所的混合气味

手指游离于身体
一颗烟独自燃烧
与灵魂构成死角
九十度的垂直
某种梦境血红
空白的背景抽搐着
大火焚烧后的树林
残存的秃枝上
烤焦的羽毛讲述春天

谈话
说笑
爵士乐模糊了面孔
烟，已经烧到了尽头
烟蒂的记忆在临终前
从新衣服的撕裂处
突然翠绿
破碎的遗骨
用来买单
侍者微笑着
赠送一个不新鲜的果盘

握手
拥抱
道别的寒暄用多种语言

A lone burning cigarette
Coffee
Ice cream
Cool cubes of ice in a whisky
Some transfixed foreigners question me
about the events of that spring day
My reply has a whiff of
a grand hotel's wash-
room mixed with a public toilet

Fingers drift away from the body
a lone cigarette burns
with the soul constructs a dead angle
90-degree perpendicular
a certain blood-red dreamscape
empty white backdrop vibrates
Forest consumed by fire
on a bare branch the scorched trace
of a feather describes that spring day

Talk
speak laugh
Jazz-blurred faces
Cigarette, almost burned down by now
filter's memory approaches its end
From within a tear in new clothes
a sudden greenness
Smashed bone remnants
used to settle the check
The waiter smiles
presents a plate of spoiled fruit

Shake hands
Embrace
Parting conventions use multiple languages

坟墓没有国籍
一只手从空酒杯 移向
最后挣扎的烟蒂
透明的烟缸展示尸体
有灰烬有口水
有夜生活的糜烂
春天很冷
我的醉意被跟踪
脚印中的窃听器
使我不敢稍做停留

古老的城市焕然一新
只有那个日子陈旧得
象致命的病毒
没有人愿意接近
我看见了亡灵
那个拉直头发的姑娘
立在马路和星光之间
车流中的迷失者
是天地间的全景
是此时此刻
仅存的生命

Graves have no nationality
A hand shifts from an empty beer glass
to the filter's final exertion
a display of corpses through a transparent ashtray
with the embers the saliva
the nightlife depravities
Spring's so cold
My drunkenness is being shadowed
footsteps wiretapped
I don't pause for a second

Ancient city glows anew
Only that one archaic date exists
like a fatal virus
no one's willing to approach
I can see the dead souls
the girl with straightened hair
standing in the starlit road
the martyrs among a stream of cars
is the landscape of heaven and earth
is this time this moment
life's only existence

1994年6月5日于北京家中

从一块石头的粉碎开始
——"六·四"五周年祭

From the Shattered Pieces of a Stone It Begins

At home in Beijing, 5/6/1994
Fifth anniversary offering for 4/6

这里
开始下陷
一块石头的粉碎
笔直且深不可测
有人疯了
逼迫大地与他一起 玩
杀人的游戏

在瞎子的眼底徘徊
围绕黑色的火焰
还没有诞生的人
先于我死去
母亲的子宫变成地狱
地狱在羊水的喂养下
变成刽子手的天堂
奥斯维辛或耶路撒冷
经过焚尸炉的冶炼
哭墙的残砖
如此坚硬
刺穿古老的历史

惊人的遗忘
帮助废墟死而复生
幸运者被腐烂滋养
一纸悔罪书
苟活了肉体
蚊虫鼓胀的尸体
粘在一面雪白的墙上
伸手拍打水泥
掌纹变成街道的裂痕
浸满了黎明的血

闭上眼睛之前
这把刀又一次雪亮
照澈内脏

This place
begins to cave
shattered pieces of stone
straight verticality into unfathomable depths
Someone's turned deranged
forces the land to play
a murderer's game

Beneath the blindman's line of sight flickers
an encircling black flame
Those unborn
die before me
A mother's womb becomes an inferno
amniotic fluid-feeding inferno
becomes an executioner's paradise
Auschwitz or Jerusalem
passes through the smelting furnace
wailing wall's stone remains
so hard
to pierce ancient history

Amazing how the forgetting
enables deathly ruins to be reborn
the fortunate nourished by the decomposed
A page of penance
the flesh lives on in degradation
Mosquito-bloated corpse
is stuck to a snow-white wall
extended hand taps cement
palm-lines turn into cracks in the street
blood floods daybreak

Before the eyes shut
this knife shines snow-
bright once more through the inner organs

如同用核武器点燃雪茄
使地球患上肺癌
向情人告别
柔软的身体里
寻找被切割的感觉
仿佛生来第一次直视
就注定毁于另一种目光

大脑中有一只鞋
找不到通向记忆的路

as using a nuclear bomb to light a cigar
sends lung cancer across the earth
to parting lovers
Inside the softness of the body
look for the severed perception
akin to the first fixed gaze after being born
soon doomed to be subsumed by another vision

In the brain-mass there's one shoe
that cannot find the road to memory

1995年6月3日于北京西北郊市公安局软禁处

记忆
——"六·四"六周年祭

Memory

*Under house arrest with the Public Security Bureau
in the northwest outskirts of Beijing, 3/6/1995
Sixth anniversary offering for 4/6*

一

夜晚
悬挂在锋利的边缘
数次醒来
想看清些什么
数次睡去如临深渊
大雾在体内弥漫
微风， 偶尔闪亮
一根针游走在血管里
连缀起支离破碎的词句
思绪破败
象离散的情人
抱怨彼此的背叛

1

Late in the night
suspended at a sheer edge
So often woken up
wanting to see what clearly
So often sleep's like facing an abyss
Thick fog spreads within the body
gentle wind, intermittent flash
a needle migrates through the veins
stitches together scattered fragments of words
Ideals' threads destroyed
like lovers torn apart
betrayed by one another's reproaches

二

为一种被流放的妄想
需要简明清晰的虚无
时光倒流如时光飞逝
血泊中的面容睁大眼睛
尘土的气味飘散开来
记忆的空白
象超级市场
今天是情人的生日
每一小时都很珍贵
必须用潇洒的
百元钞票和信用卡
添满

To serve a dream that's been exiled
requires the simple clearness of emptiness
Time flows backward as time passes on
In a pool of blood a face an eye opens wide
dust's odour lingers and disperses
Memory's white-space
like a supermarket
Today is my love's birthday
each hour so precious
necessitates the natural unrestraint
of using a hundred-yuan bill and a credit card
to add to the fullness

三

意识到自己是劫难的幸存者
我会尽力感到震惊或羞愧
意识到活下去是宿命
我几乎潸然泪下或痉挛
自由是一条名牌领带
摆放在熏香的衣柜里
尊严是一张用不完的支票
在饭店和商场之间
在银行和股市之间
千百次地传递
无数张激动的年轻面孔
曾经是旗帜是口号是标语
而一场阴雨过后
自由女神手中的火炬
变成没人念的悼词

3

Becoming conscious of being disaster's survivor
I'll strive to feel astonishment or shame
Becoming conscious that living on is karma
I'm so close to tears or convulsions
Freedom is a brand-name tie
stored in a wardrobe with incense
Honour is an inexhaustible cheque
at a hotel at the store
at a bank at the stock exchange
a hundred a thousand times transferred
Innumerable awakened young faces were once
flags were once slogans were once propaganda posters
but after the grey rain passed
the torch of the Goddess of Democracy
turned into a eulogy no one remembers

四

死者们上路时
我不曾相送
外交公寓里宽大的浴缸
浸泡着受惊吓的肉体
水的温柔能剥去皮肤
却洗不去灵魂的污垢

军车停在立交桥上燃烧
枪口对着阳台上的摄象机
蓝眼睛和黑眼睛相互对视
找不到打开家门的钥匙

是谁，偶尔拍下了
站在坦克前的小伙子
他挥手臂动
让全世界为之感动
但，除了坦克上的炮口
没人看清过他的面容
他的名字
他无人知道
后来呢后来呢
他踪迹全无
曾为他流泪的世界
也懒得再去寻找

他们上路时
还很年轻
扑倒在地的瞬间
还为一线生机抽搐挣扎

4

When the dead set out on the road
I never see them off
In the spacious bathtub of the diplomat's residence
soaks the terrified flesh
the water's gentle warmth peels the skin
but cannot wash off the soul's filth

The military vehicle on the overpass burns
guns face video cameras on a balcony
Blue eyes and dark eyes stare into each other
unable to find the key that opens the door home

Who was it, the one casually photographed
the young lad standing before the tank
waving his arms
moving the whole world
and yet, save for the tank's muzzle
no one could see his face
His name, too,
no one knows
And then . . . and then
his trace disappeared
the world that cried for him
didn't want to keep looking for him

When they set out on the road
still so young
in the instant they collapsed to the earth
there was still a thread of the struggle's trembling vitality

他们被投进焚尸炉时
身体还很柔软
无名的尸体化为灰烬
一个时代或漫长的历史
也至多是一缕青烟

When they were thrown into the furnace
flesh still soft
nameless corpses transformed into ash
the epoch or endless history
is at most a wisp of black smoke

五

生活，只是无差别的连续
一天和一年没有区别
谈恋爱和搞阴谋没有区别
抽烟、闲聊、泡酒吧
性交、搓麻、洗桑拿
贪污、跑官、贩卖人口
剥下了皮的身体
一副不辱使命的凛然
时间住进了疯人院
小康的日子很享受
金钱那么轻易地
原谅了刺刀和谎言
为屠杀辩护的理由
象儒道互补的形而上学
成为人人都接受的理想

5

Life is but continuous indifference
a day and a year are no different
To fall in love and to plot a conspiracy are no different
to smoke, gossip, barhop
have sex, play mahjong, bathe in a sauna
practise graft, scheme for office, traffic in people
Skin peeled from body
an awe-inspiring task completed
Time checked into the mental asylum
days of little comforts so pleasurable
The ease with which money
forgives bayonets and lies
to justify the massacre with reasoned arguments
like the metaphysics of Daoist-Confucius exchange
that becomes the accepted ideology for one and everyone

六

这个民族
惯于把坟墓记忆成宫殿
在有奴隶主之前
已经学会了
怎样下跪才最优美

6

This nation
is used to memorialising tombs as palaces
before slave owners existed
it was already well-learned
so as to kneel with the most exquisite grace

1996年6月2日 —— 7日于北京

我将放纵我的灵魂
——"六·四"七周年祭

I Will Give My Soul Free Rein

Beijing, 2/6 – 7/6/1996
Seventh anniversary offering for 4/6

一

我是一个残疾人
拖着被子弹射穿的腿
目光被绷带缠得太久
散发着腐烂的锋利
我的手指象我的呼吸
夹着劣质的烟草
留下有毒的灰烬
灵魂象卖淫的身体
裸露着
紧贴冰冷的石阶
地下的哭泣
被遗弃的婴儿
躺在生锈的针尖上

1

I am a cripple
dragging a bullet-maimed leg around
Gaze bound with bandages for too long
a pungent rot drifts out
My fingers like my breath
infused with cheap tobacco
that burns to toxic flecks of ash
The soul is like a prostitute's body
naked, exposed
splayed upon ice-cold steps of stone
Weeping underground
of an abandoned baby
who lies on the point of a rusted needle

二

我是残疾人
孑然一身
走进这座残疾的城市
罪恶如同点缀庆典的鲜花
无数幸存者重新抖擞
为了乞求活命的面包
把自由交给了股市
贪欲和欺骗
象汽车的尾气
污染着空气阳光和人的表情

那次革命盛宴散席后
幸运的英雄们漂洋过海
继续参加舆论和捐款的大餐
无奈留下来的精英们
来不及掩埋同伴的遗体
来不及擦净裤脚的血痕
就一头扎进了浩浩商海
留下无家可归的亡灵
象饥肠辘辘的野狗
找不到一块骨头

那次民主会餐的酒杯
被戒严的子弹击碎后
到处都是免费的饭局
身价十万元的黄金大宴
咀嚼后剩下的残渣中
还有几片从东洋进口的金箔
闪着无辜的微光

革命犹如高潮
患上精神阳痿的民族
高举着阳具满世界招摇

2

I'm a cripple
all alone
entering the crippled city
Evil's akin to the fresh, decorative flowers of a celebration
Countless survivors gather strength once more
to beg for their daily bread scraps
Hand freedom over to the stock market
Greed and deception
like the exhaust from a car
pollute the air the sunlight and human expression

After the feast of the revolution ended
the fortunate heroes crossed the oceans and seas
to continue their grand meals of public opinion and fundraising
Those educated elite with no choice but to stay
had no time to bury their fellow companions' remains
had no time to clean the traces of blood from their turn-ups
but plunged headfirst into the vast seas of trade
The departed souls with no home to return to
became like wild dogs stomachs rumbling
unable to find a single bone

Beer glasses of democracy activists
shattered by bullets during martial law
Everywhere there are free banquets, grand
feasts of gold that cost one hundred thousand yuan a head
sediment-remains after chewing
contain imported gold leaf from Japan
reflecting the glimmer of the innocents

The revolution is like an orgasm
and the nation suffering from spiritual impotence
shows off its raised prick to the world

当着妻子的面
几个男人
满口酒气地交流着
嫖娼时积累的经验
局长、大款、作家和学者
争相攀比的不是钱与名
而是谁的鸡巴
能够坚挺不倒
从午夜到世纪末的黎明
从泰国海滨到纽约第七十二街

In front of their wives
some guys
breath full of beer exchange
well-experienced stories of visiting whores
Bureau chief, tycoon, author, scholar
clash with each other if not over money then fame
And yet whose cock
can stay firm and erect, not topple
from midnight to the dawn of the next century
from Thailand to New York's 72nd Street

三

我僵硬在混沌之中
不敢移动不敢弯腰
任卑琐在身边起落
任猥亵穿透心脏
人们的微笑很纯洁
只闪着人民币的光
命中注定的殉难之路
与妓女唇印叠在一起
呻吟和泣血也轻浮放荡
需要可口可乐来解渴
江核心的主旋律
残存的暴力句法
在港台的软语包装下
是小康时代的文化口红

一个八十年代的先锋作家
冲着中南海的红墙撒尿
"为人民服务"的腥臊
变成BBC的头条
他又和洋倒爷勾肩搭背
进口一批漏气的避孕套
不朽的红色幽默
魅力来自精巧的唇舌
象一把切蛋糕的小刀
甜蜜地割下人的尊严
萨义德沉重地叹气
东方主义复活了孔子
在坟墓中放了一个
振兴中华的长屁
啊!
腰身好舒展呀!
逝者如斯
危难中的华夏大地

3

I stiffen in the chaos
dare not move, dare not bend down
let base trifles rise and fall beside the body
let decadence pierce the heart
Everyone's smile is so pure
flashing a *Renmenbi* lustre
Life's fated path of the sacrificed
and a hooker's hickeys overlap
The groans of pain the tears of blood and the empty
debaucheries need Coca-Cola to slake
Jiang Zemin's core theme
a remnant of violent syntax
with Hong Kong-Taiwan packaged euphemisms
the lipstick of culture in this age of little comforts

A pioneering author of the 1980s
pisses on Zhongnanhai's red wall
'Serve the People' stench of urine
becomes a BBC headline
He then rubs shoulders with a foreign speculator
to import condoms that leak
Immortal red humour
spins an exquisite argument
as a dull cake-cutting knife
sweetly slices a person's dignity
Edward Said sighs gravely
Confucius resurrected by orientalism
in his grave breaks
the long wind of Chinese nation revitalisation
Ahhh!
the waist so relaxed slackens out!
Passing away as the river passes
land of Cathay disaster

此刻是多么需要
腐朽的资本主义
垂死的共产主义
没落的封建主义

How the moment now needs
capitalism to decompose
communism to die
feudalism to sink

四

我家简陋的住房
紧邻着李鹏的深宅大院
通向万寿路一号的柏油路
与宽阔的长安街比起来
象一条乡村小道
每天的某个时刻
这里站满了警察
所有的车辆必须绕行
让黑色的"奔驰"驶过
车里的人正在打盹
梦见儿子携巨款外逃

经常是皎洁的月光下
经过这里的车
都要接受突然的盘问
路两边的树杆上
反铐着男男女女
他们说不清彼此的关系
描了眼影的
被怀疑为妓女
拿着手机的
被认定为嫖客
武警的钢盔吸引了星光
恐惧穿透夜的血管
红指甲绿指甲蓝指甲
无法引诱坚强的战士
只有印着领袖像的大钞票
能够用乞求的表情
收买这样的夜晚

4

My crude apartment building neighbours
Li Peng's opulent linked-courtyard residence
Compared to the wide expanse of Chang'an Avenue
the tarmac that leads to 1 Wanshou Road
is a little rustic trail
At a certain time each day
this place fills with policemen
and all vehicles must detour away
to let the black Benz speed by as
the passenger inside dozes off and dreams
of his son fleeing abroad with a fortune

Often, beneath the purity of moonlight
the cars that pass here
are stopped for random interrogation
Men and women are handcuffed to the trunks
of trees on both sides of the avenue
They have no idea what each person has to do with the other
Those with eyeshadow
are suspected of being prostitutes
Those with cell phones
are determined to be their clients
Starlight's attracted to the steel helmets of the military police
fear pierces the blood vessels of the night
Red nails green nails blue nails
the hardened soldiers cannot be seduced
Only the large bills printed with our leaders' images
can be used with a beggar's expression
to bribe this manner of night

五

黑暗统治的城市
早已告别了
被勒住咽喉的黎明
又一次迎来
被茅台、XO 和精液浸透的夜晚

在这座无耻得
接近完美的城市里
一切都被包装
只有残忍是透明的
纯粹的透明

在这个正义也要靠
广告上的大腿推销的时代
自我亵渎的人
得到太阳的加冕
仪式的盛大得如同
剥了皮的甜橙
绽开橘黄的嫩肉
享受着失去味觉的舌头

我是一个残疾人
无力逃脱
这样的城市这样的时代
唯一的庆幸
我还有被放逐的灵魂
它没有腿没有眼睛
却能够拄着双拐
不辩方向
也不避风雨
四处流浪

5

Bid farewell to the dark
regime's city long ago
Throat-throttled dawn
welcomed back again, night
soaked with Maotai XO and semen

In this city of near perfect
shamelessness
everything's packaged
Only brutality is transparent
a transparent purity

In this righteous yet dependent age
of bared-thigh-selling ads
the self-abused
have reached the crown of the sun
The resplendent ritual is like
a sweet tangerine peeled of its skin
soft orange flesh erupts, savoured
by a tongue that has lost its sense of taste

I am a cripple
powerless to escape
this city this age where
there's only one thing to celebrate:
I still have an exiled soul
It has neither legs nor eyes
but can lean on a pair of crutches
doesn't dispute which way
nor evades wind and rain
in the four directions drifts with the waves

1997年6月4日凌晨于大连市劳动教养院

那个日子
——"六·四"八周年祭

That Day

Before dawn at the re-education through labour camp
in Dalian, 4/6/1997
Eighth anniversary offering for 4/6

那个日子
是一种疾病
从祖先初次乱伦后
它便遗传下来
潜伏在皇帝精子中
作为命运
那个日子选择了
没有免疫力的子孙
女娲用泥土造人和补天
精卫用生命填海
谭嗣同的身首异处
也无法挽回
一个民族的健康

五千年的不治之症
突然有了一剂良药

那个日子
给懦弱的骨头
唯一一次坚强的机会
从一面镜子到整个天空
再也找不到
欣赏阿Q式虚荣的理由

那个日子的绝望
把我们逼到了
没有任何退路的悬崖
粉身碎骨的瞬间
就是疾病痊愈的时刻

如果在创世的混沌中
我们曾把自己当作人
圣贤的教诲使我们
有骄傲有敬畏有谦卑
如果在屠刀下

That day
was a disease
passed down from the ancestors' first
incestuous act through the genes
lurked in the Emperor's sperm
as destiny
That day had been set
offspring without immunity
Nüwa used earth to make humans and mend heaven
Jingwei used her bird-life to fill the sea
Tan Sitong's decapitation
couldn't redeem
the health of a nation

5,000 years of an incurable disease
then a sudden dose of good medicine

That day
gave craven bones
only one solid chance
From a mirror's surface to the sky's expanse
no reason can be found again
to admire an Ah Q-pattern of vanity

That day's desperation
forced us toward a precipice
with no path of escape
The blink of bodies being crushed bones smashed
occurred at the moment the disease was retreating

If in creation's innocence
we once considered ourselves human
and the sages' teachings gave us
pride gave us reverence gave us humility
if beneath the butcher's knife

我们 拥抱过情人的尸体
为什么那个日子的尖锐
能擦亮全世界的目光
却惟独刺不痛我们的眼睛
为什么那个日子的手臂
从子夜举到黎明
从鲜红举到紫黑
我们却爬向刽子手的脚下

被扒光的男男女女
从焚尸炉的青烟中站起
草草地梳洗一下，甚至
来不及对镜自恋
就匆匆步入五星级酒店
去服侍豪华套间的大床
微笑得那么精致准确
象秦始皇陵展示的
令人叹为观止的铜马车

我们疾病又发作了
那是从未体验过的享受
丢失了灵魂的我们
庆幸只剩下肉体
发达的四肢已经足够
彻底的唯物主义者无所畏惧
我们不是上帝的造物
从不用担心末日的审判
我们的疾病多美呀
西施的美林黛玉的美
根植于这种疾病

上帝又能怎样
有上帝的白种人
也有撒旦
每天进教堂忏悔的金发

we had embraced our beloved's corpse
why did the keen blade of that day
illuminate the whole world's gaze
yet our eyes alone were pierced without pain
Why did our arms that day
raise from midnight to first light
raise from bright red to bruised black
and yet we still crawled toward the executioner's feet

Men and women stripped bare
stand up in the dark smoke of the incinerator
wash up, dress in haste, too rushed to even
admire themselves in the mirror
just hurry into the five star hotel
to tend to the huge bed of the luxury suite
with a satisfied smile so exquisitely exact
like the bronze chariot of Qin Shi Huang's Tomb
that steals people's breath away

Our disease breaks out again
From a pleasure we had never experienced before
our soul was lost
luckily the flesh was left
development of the four limbs sufficient
to become a devoted materialist free of all fears
Yet we are not God's creation
never having to worry about the Day of Judgment
Ahhh . . . how beautiful our disease
Xi Shi's beauty Lin Daiyu's beauty
both rooted in this disease

What more can God do
The God of the white race exists
as does their Devil
Each day the golden-haired ones go to church to repent

不也得了爱滋病
那炼狱的烈火不是只能
徒劳地燃烧
白白地浪费
统治世界的互连网
治不了这个绝症

唉呀呀
我们是无产者
除了锁链
我们一无所有
多么令人骄傲的赤贫
没有眼睛没有耳朵
没有嘴巴没有皮肤
没有心灵没有记忆
一无所有的无产者
只有那个日子那种疾病
白种人最致命的病
怎么能与我们相比
那么年轻的爱滋
才有几十年的历史
而我们的疾病古老得
远远超出耶稣的诞辰

再说了
爱滋病太浅薄
还需要性交
没有一点点道义感召力
而我们的疾病多深刻
学而时习之
养得浩然之气
顿悟成佛
无知者无畏
无产者无耻
从孔夫子到郭沫若

but could they not have AIDS too
The purgatorial blaze of suffering isn't just
a futile burning
a vain-white waste
the internet which reigns the world
cannot cure this terminal illness

Aiya ya ya . . .
We are the proletariat
save for chains
we have nothing
so proud in naked poverty
without eyes without ears
without a mouth without skin
a proletariat who has nothing
but that day that disease
How could such a fatally feared illness
of the white race compare with our disease
AIDS is so young
with only a few decades of history
but our disease is so ancient, exceeds
Christ's birth by a great temporal distance

Some say
AIDS is too shallow
needing sex, not presuming
the slightest moral inspiration
whereas our disease is so deep
takes learning with constant practice
grows with righteous airs
in a flash of Buddha-insight
the fearlessness of the ignorant
the shamelessness of the proletariat
from Confucius to Guo Moruo

从三皇五帝到唐宗宋祖
从贞女烈妇到文臣武将
从毛泽东到邓小平
从圣贤到引车卖浆之流

· ·

我们这个民族
能够用那种疾病抵御一切
我们每个人
都要在子宫中学习无耻
而无耻者才能做到
真正的无畏——
从践踏生命到亵渎神灵

我们轻易挥霍了那个日子
如同我们从未有过那种疾病

from the Three Sovereigns Five Emperors to the Tang-Song Kings
from the virtuous virgins martyred widows to the court officials
    military generals
from Mao Zedong to Deng Xiaoping
from the sages to the street-cart vendors and on and on

. . . .

For this nation of ours
to use this disease as a mass resistance
we must each one
learn shamelessness in the womb
and then the shameless will become
truly fearless –
from trampling on life to blaspheming the gods

We who effortlessly squandered that day
as if we had never suffered such a disease

1998年6月4日凌晨于大连市劳动教养院

又逼近并击穿
——"六·四"九周年祭

Closing in and Breaking Through

Before dawn at the re-education through labour camp
*   in Dalian, 4/6/1998*
Ninth anniversary offering for 4/6

菜盆中苍蝇的尸体
被我细细地咀嚼后
吐向残红的黄昏
一群秃头在操场上
随着口令重复同一个动作
等待就要到来的检查
电视中的赵本山或宋祖英
同屋人的大笑或聊天
他们熟悉所有的明星
最喜欢哼着"心太软"
去摸屏幕上的乳房和屁股

我仍然坐在角落里
给妻子写第 609 封信
文字突然昏厥
胃的痉挛左右了笔尖
几乎是本能地感到
那个时辰又逼近了
从划破的纸张的反面
击穿我脑后的反骨
那块每晚被妻子
温存爱抚的反骨
那块在初中一年级时
被群专的小号囚禁
被棍棒砖头砸击的
反骨

被击穿的时刻
坟墓一定很孤独
纵使我有勇气
再一次坐牢
也没有足够的勇气
挖掘记忆中的尸体

The dead flies in the pan of food
I finely grind and chew then
spit at the withering-red dusk
A group of shaved-headed ones in the courtyard
follow repeated commands with the same synchronised
actions while awaiting the expected inspections
Zhao Benshan comedy or Song Zuying singing on TV
Cellmates laugh aloud and chatter
they're familiar with all the shows' stars
like most to croon Richie Ren's 'Too Softhearted'
rise to touch tits and ass on the screen

I continue to sit in a corner
to write letter 609 to my wife
Script abruptly goes faint
stomach spasm makes the pen-point falter
It's practically an instinctive feeling
the hour closes in again
from the reverse side of the slashed piece of paper
breaks through the bone into the back of my brain
the rebellious bone that has yet to finish
spiriting tender caresses to my wife
that in the first year of middle school
caused a group of us nobodies to be imprisoned
that beaten-by-stick-and-brick of a
rebellious spirit-
bone

Moment broken
graves a fixed loneliness
Even if I have the courage
to be jailed again
it isn't courage enough
to dig up corpses from memory

如同我不敢
吞下嚼烂了的苍蝇

死亡埋葬了正义之后
已经抛弃了死亡

地下的孩子们
腐烂得只剩下发丝
纤细的哭泣偷偷飞翔
使晴朗的夜晚雨雪弥漫
天空的心脏停止跳动
犹如未婚先孕的子宫里
怀上一堆石头和冰块
为了逃避人工流产
在母腹中
婴儿学会了自杀

我再一次拒绝进食
掏空身体，也无法
走进信仰的废墟
当百合花找不到泥土时
拼凑反骨的碎片
栽种在海上
盐的追悼和守侯

今夜，梦中没有情人
却有一只发抖的蚂蚁
刺刀尖戳进洞穴
惊醒蚁群
蚂蚁也许不知道
大屠杀意味着什么
但是，当有智慧的生物
都在遗忘中渐渐麻木时
蚂蚁那颤栗的记忆
使大地完整

as I dare not swallow
those mashed flies

When death has buried justice
the dead have long been abandoned

Children in the ground
decompose to wisps of hair
faint weeping surreptitiously soars up
fills the clear night with rain and snow
The heart of the sky stops beating
as if a heap of rocks and ice was conceived
within an unmarried woman's pregnant womb
In order to escape the abortion
the baby inside mother's belly
learns how to commit suicide

Once more I refuse to eat
hollowing the body, unable
to enter the ruins of belief
When the white lily cannot find a patch of dirt
gather the rebellious fragments of spirit-
bone and plant them in the sea
a eulogy an expectation of salt

Tonight, there's no beloved in my dreams
just a mass of trembling ants
bayonet point pierces a cavernous hole
waking the swarm
Perhaps the ants aren't aware
of what a massacre means
and yet these living beings must possess some form
of intelligence, as a creeping numbness takes over
in the forgetting, the ants' shuddering
memory makes the Earth whole

1999年6月4日凌晨于大连市劳动教养院

站在时间的诅咒中
——"六·四"十周年祭

Standing in the Curse of Time

Before dawn at the re-education through labour camp
in Dalian, 4/6/1999
Tenth anniversary offering for 4/6

站在时间的诅咒中
那个日子格外陌生

一

十年前的这一天
黎明，一件血衣
太阳，被撕碎的日历
所有的目光都停留在
这唯一的一页
世界化为一个悲愤的凝视
时间不能容忍天真
死者们抗争着呐喊着
直到泥土的喉咙
嘶哑

攥住监室中的铁条
这一刻
我必须放声大哭
我多么害怕下一刻
已经欲哭无泪
记住无辜的死
必须在眼睛正中
冷静地插进一把刺刀
用失明的代价
换取脑浆的雪亮
那种敲骨吸髓的记忆
只有以拒绝的方式
才能完美地表达

Standing in the curse of time
that day seems so unfamiliar

1

Ten years ago this day's
dawn: a bloody garment
sun: calendar torn to shreds
All eyes stop
at this single page
the world becomes a sorrowful indignant gaze
Time cannot tolerate the blameless
dead who resist and shout
until their throats turn to a dirt-
filled hoarseness

Grasping the iron bars of the cell
this very moment
I must howl with tears
so afraid I am of the next
moment now grief without tears
To remember the innocent dead
calmly stick a bayonet
into the eye's centre
and use the price of blindness
to restore the brain's snowbrightness
That bone-crushing marrow-sucking
memory which only by means of refusal
can be perfectly expressed

二

十年后的这一天
训练有素的士兵
以最标准最庄严的姿势
护卫着那个弥天大谎
五星红旗就是黎明
在晨光中迎风飘扬
人们掂起脚、伸长脖
好奇、惊诧和虔诚
一个年轻的母亲
举起怀中孩子的小手
向遮住天空的谎言致敬

而另一个白发母亲
吻着遗像中的儿子
她掰开儿子的每个手指
仔细清洗指甲中的血污
她找不到一捧泥土
让儿子在地下得到宁静
她只能把儿子挂在墙上

这位走遍无名墓的母亲
为了揭穿一个世纪的谎言
从被勒紧的喉咙中
抠出那些窒息了的名字
让自己的自由和尊严
作为对遗忘的控诉
被警察跟踪和窃听

2

Ten years later today's
well-trained soldiers
a most official most stately posturing
guard that wholly monstrous lie
Red five-starred flag in dawn's
morning light flutters in the wind
People rise up on their feet, stretch their necks high
so strange, such stunned reverence
A young mother holds her child
to her chest and raises its little hand
to salute the lie that blots out the sky

A different mother hair greyed
kisses a photograph of her dead son
She pries open each of his fingers
to gently wash the dried blood beneath his nails
She's unable to find a handful of dirt
to give her son peace beneath earth
She just hangs her son up onto the wall

This mother of a nameless grave who walks on
and on to expose a world's lie
with throat constricted forces out
the suffocated names
to turn her own freedom and dignity
into a denouncement of forgetting
that tails and wiretaps the police

三

这个世界上最大的广场
已经被翻修一新

山沟里出来的刘邦
做了汉高祖之后
用母亲与神龙私通
演义家族的荣耀
多么古老的轮回
从长陵到纪念堂
刽子手都被庄严安葬
在豪华的地下宫殿里
隔着几千年的历史
昏君和暴君之间
一边讨论刺刀的智慧
一边接受陪葬者的跪拜

再过几个月
这里将举行盛大的庆典
纪念堂中保存完好的尸体
做着皇帝梦的刽子手
将共同检阅
走过天安门的杀人工具
如同秦始皇在坟墓中
检阅不朽的兵马俑

此刻，那个阴魂
回味着生前的辉煌
那些坐吃山空的后代
将在阴魂的保佑下
用白骨铸成的权杖
祈祷新世纪更美好

3

This city square the largest in the world
has been rebuilt anew

Liu Bang who emerged from the ravine
after becoming the Great Ancestor of Han
used the romance between his mother
and the divine dragon to glorify the family clan
How ancient is reincarnation
from the Chang Ling Tomb to the Mausoleum
All the executioners have been solemnly interred
in luxurious underground palaces
Separated by ten thousand years of history
the fatuous sovereign and the tyrannical sovereign
on one side discuss the wisdom of the bayonet
on the other receive the prostrations of those who'll be buried

After several months
there will be a grand celebration
the well-preserved corpse of the Mausoleum
and the executioner dreaming of being Emperor
shall together inspect the marching
of the murderous instruments of Tiananmen
as if Qin Shi Huang in his tomb
inspecting his immortal terracotta army

Now, the wraith reflects
upon the glory of his living days
The later generations of eating-mountains-of-emptiness
will be bestowed with the wraith's blessing
as he forges a rod of power out of a bone's whiteness
and prays for an even more beautiful new century

在鲜花和坦克之中
在敬礼和刺刀之中
在鸽子和导弹之中
在整齐的步伐和麻木的表情之中
旧世纪的结束
只有血腥的黑暗
新世纪的开始
没有一丝生命之光

Between the flower and the tank
between the salute and the bayonet
between the dove and the missile
between the ordered step and the numbed expression
the old century ends
Only the stench of a blood-spilt darkness
opens the new century
without a thread of life shining out

四

拒绝进食
停止手淫
从废墟上拣起一本书
惊叹尸体的谦卑
在蚊子的内脏里
做着黑红的梦
靠近铁门的监视孔
与吸血鬼交谈
不必再那么小心翼翼
突然的胃痉挛
给我临终前的勇气
呕出一个诅咒
五十年的辉煌
只有共产党
没有新中国

4

Refused to eat
Stopped masturbating
Picked up a book from the ruins
Marvel at a corpse's humility
Within a mosquito's internal organs
a dark-red dream
approaches a spy-hole in the iron door
Converse with a vampire
No need to be so covert so cautious anymore
A sudden stomach spasm
gives me the courage before death
to spew out a curse:
Fifty years of glory
there's only the Communist Party
and no sign of the New China-y

2001年1月17日于北京家中

献给苏冰娴先生
——"六·四"十一周年祭

For Su Bingxian

At home in Beijing, 17/1/2001
Eleventh anniversary offering for 4/6

一

你突然离去的噩耗
正值冬季少有的大雪
为肮脏的北京
披上伪装的时辰
天安门广场上执勤的武警
用皮靴踢碎了
一个孩子堆起的雪人

十一年前
你的孩子
就像这个雪人
被罪恶的子弹击碎
枪声响过之后
恐惧在每一个大脑
安装了监听器
叹息和泪水也被录音

1

The sudden news of your passing
arrived in winter with a rare heavy snowfall
that draped the foulness of Beijing
in a temporary disguise
At Tiananmen Square an armed policeman on
watch used his leather boot to kick and break
apart a child's snowman piled up high

11 years ago
your child your son
was just like that snowman
smashed by the pure wretchedness of bullets
After the echoes of gunfire
fear spread through everyone's minds
Surveillance devices also recorded
the wails and the weeping

二

不许悼念
不许追忆
不许失去儿子的母亲
和失去丈夫妻子见面
不许高位截瘫的小伙子
坐著轮椅，接受
一次尝试行走的搀扶
不许寡母
接受一束鲜花
不许孤儿
得到一个新书包
不许任何温暖的手
为无家可归的冤魂
添一捧土种一株草
更不许所剩无几的眼睛
寻找刽子手的藏身之处
不许不许不许不许……
十一年前
不许一滴雨
落在龟裂的土地上
十一年后
不许孩子堆起的雪人
有短暂生命

2

Forbidden to grieve
Forbidden to recollect
Forbidden for the mother who lost her son
to visit the wife who lost her husband
Forbidden for the young paraplegic
sitting in a wheelchair, to receive
an arm of support for him to walk
Forbidden for the widow
to receive a bouquet of flowers
Forbidden for the orphan
to be given a new book-bag
Forbidden for warm hands to help
the wronged ghost with no home to return to
with just a handful of dirt to plant a green patch
Strictly forbidden for the few forlorn eyes left
to seek the executioners in their lawful hiding-places
Forbidden forbidden forbidden forbidden . . .
11 years ago
it was forbidden for a drop of rain
to fall on this cracked tortoise-shell earth
11 years later
it is forbidden for the snowman the child piled
up to live out its brief life

三

雪下著
一代代冤魂
堆积起来
那冰清玉洁
看上去是虚幻的假相
太阳一出来
成顿的垃圾
填满记忆

刺刀能够
劈开身体和影子
割断雪花和大地
却割不断烛光和夜晚
任何形式的祭奠
于那曾经热的血
都过于苍白
是母亲的皱纹
让鲜血变成满天大雪
以坟墓的姿态飞翔

3

Snowfall
generation after generation
of wronged ghosts pile up
The ice-clear jade pureness
is an illusory semblance
When the sun comes out
heaps of trash
flood memory full

A bayonet
can cleave body from shadow
sever snowflake from earth
yet cannot split apart the candle flames from the night
Any form of memorial
for what was once impassioned blood
is inevitably too pale
The wrinkles of the Mothers
turn spilt blood into snow-thick skies
for the figures of the graves to soar into

四

关于死亡
我能说的
决不会多于
你临终前的眼睛
每一瞥带来的震撼
决不亚于一次
末日审判

4

Concerning death
whatever I say
can be no more than
your eyes just before dying
each stirring-still glance
will be no less than the first
last day of judgment

2001年5月30日于北京家中

一块木板的记忆
——"六·四"十二周年祭

Memories of a Wooden Plank

At home in Beijing, 30/5/2001
Twelfth anniversary offering for 4/6

我是一块木板
一寸半厚的长方形木板
被遗弃的命运，让我
和一个年轻人的相遇
坦克与血肉对峙
细致的木纹保存了
那个被惊呆的黎明
那个被子弹逼进死胡同的黎明

长安街抽搐时
我也跟着震颤
履带碾过我的一角
植物纤维发出挤压后
断裂的嘶叫
我想躲避想逃走
我知道　钢铁比我坚硬
但，我，不能！

傍边，不远的地方
一堆已经模糊的肉体
离我太近，头正中
裂开一个大洞
很深很黑，血腥
已渗入木纹深处
豆腐脑一样雪白的
那是什么？

那是什么？我不知道
我想他比我勇敢
像我出生地的顽石
可他比我脆弱比我痛
是我庇护下的小草
我要救他

I am a wooden plank
a one-and-a-half-inch thick rectangular plank
abandoned to fate, let me
and the youth cross paths
to confront the tanks with flesh and blood
Delicate grain of wood has preserved
the stunned dawn
the forced-by-bullets-into-a-blind-alley dawn

As Chang'an Avenue shudders
I, too, tremble
Chained treads crush one of my corners
woody fibres squeeze out
then a rupturing shriek
I want to hide, I want to flee
knowing steel is stronger than me
but . . . I . . . cannot!

To the side, nearby
a vague viscous pile of bodies
and too near to me, a head
with a large punctured hole
so deep so dark, the stench
of blood soaks through the wood-grain
that stuff as snow-white as beancurd jelly
what *is* it?

What is it? I don't know
I think he's braver than me
like the unfeeling stone of my birthplace
though he's more fragile than me suffers more than me
the young sprout I protect
I want to save him

那些与他一样的生命
逃吧逃吧　越快越好
他们比我年轻
面对坦克履带
他们比我脆弱
逃得越远越好
还未成熟的小草

来吧! 已经
无力逃走的年轻人
躺在我满是污垢的身上
我仅仅是
一块被丢弃的木板
无力抗拒钢铁的碾压
但，我要救你
无论是尸体还是奄奄一息

来吧! 头上
被炸开了大洞的年轻人
我在你瞪大的眼睛里
看见一堆堆钢铁冲过来的疯狂
那些驾驶坦克的士兵
甚至比你还年轻

来吧! 刚才
还和同伴手挽手
向着黑色的炮口和枪口
挥动手臂的年轻人
闭上你凝望天空的眼睛
用血用白色脑浆
把我和四肢残损的你
粘在一起
紧紧的

Those who share his fate
flee and flee   the faster the better
They're younger than me
facing the treads of tanks
They're more fragile than me
the farther they flee the better
young sprouts yet to mature

Come! already
powerless to flee, the youth
lies down on my filthy body
I am merely
a discarded wooden plank
powerless to resist the crushing of steel
still, I want to save you no matter if you're
dead or still barely breathing, breathing

Come! youth
with the large hole blown through your head
Inside your wide-open eyes I see
wave after wave of steel-razing madness
the soldiers driving the tanks
even younger than you

Come! a moment ago
hand in hand among friends
facing the darkness of cannon and gun
Arm-waving youth
close your sky-turned eyes
use blood use the brain's whiteness
to bind me and your broken-limbed self
together tightly
together

我想倾听
最后的心跳说些什么
我想抚摸
碎裂的皮肤下
正在冷却的血液里
残留的最后一丝体温
如果可能，把这温暖
带给你最牵挂的女友

来吧！开阔得
像天空一样的年轻人
没有云雨没有飞鸟
如果可能
让我载你回家
如果来不及
让我们就这样
一动不动，紧紧偎依
一同被钢铁碾成粉末
落入柏油路的裂缝中
在北京在六部口
在托起长安街的泥土中
变成常春藤
保存记忆

来吧！坚强如水的年轻人
如果你的亲人同意
把我做成简陋的棺椁
陪你一起入土
我的根我的家在大地深处
陪你一直睁着眼睛
在地下等待
直到你瞑目的那一天
长成森林

I want to listen to
your heartbeat's last whisper
I want to feel
beneath your ruptured skin
the cooling bloodflow's final
temperate degree
and if possible, take that trace
of warmth to your grieving girlfriend

Come! youth
opening out like the sky
without rain clouds without birds
if possible
let me carry you back home
and if it's too late
let me simply move-
not-move, ever so tightly nestle in
together crushed by steel into dust
that falls into the fissures of asphalt
in Beijing at the entrance to the Six Ministries
into the soil beds along Chang'an Avenue
transforms into perennial-spring ivy
preserver of memory

Come! youth as indomitable as water
if your loved ones agree
shape me into a crude coffin
that accompanies you into the ground
My roots my family within the depths of the earth
accompanies your always-open eyes
waiting underground until the day
your gaze can fade
into the fullness of a forest

2002年5月20日于北京家中

六四，一座坟墓
——"六·四"十三周年祭

June Fourth, a Tomb

At home in Beijing, 20/5/2002
Thirteenth anniversary offering for 4/6

守卫着权杖兵马俑
让世界为之惊叹
比宫殿还堂皇的十三陵
让西洋人错愕
毛泽东的纪念堂
修筑在奴隶的心脏正中
我们漫长的历史
全靠帝王的坟墓显示辉煌

而六四
一座没有墓碑的坟墓
一座把耻辱刻进整个民族和全部历史
的坟墓

十三年
时间是下流的炫耀
每个黎明从谎言开始
每个夜晚以贪婪结束

小康前景，原谅了一切罪恶
梦游在腐烂之中
直到躯壳化为空气
饭局上的诅咒也象赞美
一切又被再次包装
只有残忍是透明的
纯粹的透明
是一种难得的幸福

六四，一座坟墓
一座被遗忘所荒凉的坟墓

这个广场，看上去很完美
被茅台 XO 鲍鱼宴
被仪式报告三代表
被二奶精液红指甲

Of the Terracotta Army's guarding rod of power
let the world stare in wonder and compare
to the palatial magnificence of the Thirteen Tombs
let westerners be stunned
by Mao Zedong's Mausoleum
constructed in the hearts of the slaves
Our endless history depends
on the tombs of the emperors to demonstrate glory

But June Fourth
a tomb without epitaph
a carved-into-the-nation-and-history disgrace
of a tomb

13 years
time is a display of obscenities
each dawn begins with a lie
each night ends in avarice

Life's little comforts have pardoned the crimes
sleepwalking through the decay
the shell of the body turns into air
the banquet's curse is like a eulogy
everything is repackaged again
only brutality is transparent
a transparent purity
is a rare happiness

June Fourth, a tomb
a turned-desolate-from-forgetting tomb

This public square appears so perfect
with Maotai XO abalone feasts
with ceremonial reports of the Three Represents
with mistresses semen red nails

被假烟假酒假文凭
被警车钢盔电鸡巴
翻修一新

当年绝食到奄奄一息的学生
如今，可能带着儿子
在这里悠闲地放风筝
人民大会堂正灯火通明
庆祝共青团的八十诞辰
年轻的代表们根本不知道
在门外的台阶上
曾有过三个同样年轻的学生
长跪不起
也绝不会不知到
当年的大会堂里
插着输氧管的绝食学生代表
和屠夫之间的唇枪舌剑

· · · · · · · · · · · · · · · · · · · ·

不知道不知道就是不知道
历史算什么，当下才是关键
衰老的报告和年轻的笑容
环形吊灯旋转着核心
新一代北大人清华人
向谎言和强权报以经久不息的掌声
他们的前途已经铺满金币

六四，一座坟墓
一座被恐怖监控的坟墓

十三年并不漫长
却在我的脚下
断裂成无底深渊
刺进脚心的一根针
雪亮和锋利已不复存在

with fake cigarettes fake beer fake diplomas
with police cars steel helmets vibrators
revitalising it anew

That year hunger-striking students neared their last breath
Today, you can bring your son here
and fly a kite with leisure
The Great Hall of the People ablaze with lights
as the Communist Youth League celebrates its eightieth birthday
The young delegates could never know
that on the steps outside those doors
three young students like them
once fell to their knees refusing to rise
They absolutely could never know
that in the General Assembly Hall that year
hunger-striking student delegates needed oxygen tubes
while fighting the butchers with words

. . . .

Never know never know precisely never know
the worth of history when what really counts
is an archaic report and a youthful smile
Ringed chandelier revolves round the core
of a new generation of Beida and Qinghua graduates
Lies and power are greeted with endless applause
their future already paved with gold

June Fourth, a tomb
an under-terrifying-surveillance tomb

13 years really isn't so long
and yet at my feet
a bottomless abyss splits open
the arch-piercing needle, snow-
bright and sharp, doesn't exist anymore

斑驳的锈迹布满血液
心的行走
需要拐杖
如同荒凉的墓地
需要绿色
而扫墓的人
却找不到通向亡灵的路

所有的道路都被封闭
所有的眼泪都被监控
所有的鲜花都被跟踪
所有的记忆都被清洗
所有的墓碑仍是空白
刽子手的恐惧
必须由恐怖来安抚

六四,一座坟墓
一座让尸体保存生命的坟墓

被刺刀砍下的手指
被子弹穿透的头颅
被坦克碾碎的身躯
被围追堵截的悼念
而活着的人
饕餮着淫乱着
欺骗着独裁着
暴富着小康着
屈膝着乞讨着
的人
一个个正在腐烂

六四,一座坟墓
一座永不瞑目的坟墓

splotches of rust cover spilt blood
The heart needs
crutches to walk
like a desolate cemetery
needs greenness but the grave-
sweepers cannot find the road
to the departed souls

All roadways are blocked
All tears are under surveillance
All fresh flowers are shadowed
All memories are purged
All tombstones are still blank
The fears of the executioners
must be appeased through terror

June Fourth, a tomb
a let-the-dead-preserve-life tomb

Hands sliced off by bayonets
heads punctured by bullets
bodies pulverised by tanks
those in mourning pursued encircled seized
while the living
the gluttonous the promiscuous
the deceitful the despotic
the nouveau riche the well-off
the submissive the begging
people
one by one are rotting

June Fourth, a tomb
an eyes-never-to-close-in-peace tomb

在遗忘和恐怖之下
这个日子被埋葬
在记忆和勇气之中
这个日子永远活着
是不死的石头
而石头，可以呐喊
是让墓地长青的野草
而野草，可以飞翔
刺进心脏正中的刀尖
让滴血的记忆雪亮

Beneath the forgetting and the terror
this day's been buried
In memory and bravery
this day lives forever
It is an immortal stone
and though stone, can cry out
It is the grave's wild grass growing eternal green
and though wild grass, it can take flight
The blade-tip that pierces the heart's centre drips
with the blood of snowbright memory

2003年5月26日于北京家中

在亡灵目光的俯视下
——"六·四"十四周年祭

Beneath the Gaze of the Departed Souls

At home in Beijing, 26/5/2003
Fourteenth anniversary offering for 4/6

眼角挤进一道冤魂的目光
那看不见的伤口
一种突然被撕裂的思想
用忐忑的声音
讲述坟墓中的故事

压抑了太久
那秘密的预谋
仍然禁闭在谎言的堂皇之中
伤痕累累的目光
无法笔直地注视
历尽无数曲折
才能在黑暗里偶尔闪亮
洞彻荒芜灵魂的角落

一笔旧债埋葬在无辜的眼底
犹如童年的习作压在抽屉尽头

那一刻，世界是一只无力自卫的羔羊
被赤裸的太阳宰杀
上帝也惊愕得无言以对
只能默默流泪或叹息
随之而来的交易
血迹被金钱打扫干净
精神的毁灭点缀著世纪末的盛大庆典
被剥了皮的尸体
不断加入独裁权力的游行队伍
庆典从血腥开始到人肉筵席的杯盘狼藉
世纪末的罪恶和耻辱
正在繁花似锦深处
高呼"民族伟大复兴"的誓言

SARS来了
病毒弥漫在空气之中
天子脚下是惊惶失措的逃散

Eye's corner catches the gaze
of a wronged ghost, that unseen
open wound, an ideal abruptly torn apart
in an agitated voice
it tells the story of the tomb

For too long that secret
premeditated act has been repressed
locked within a magnificent lie
Gaze slashed and scarred
unable to focus straight
after so many winding difficulties
can one sometimes light up the darkness
and clearly see the desolate corner of the soul

An old debt buried before the eyes of the innocent
like a child's drawings stuffed into the back of a drawer

In that moment, the world was a defenceless lamb
slaughtered by a naked red sun
Even God watched dazed and speechless
one could only weep and sigh with silence
Then the agreement followed
washing the bloodstains clean with money
Spiritual devastation adorned the grand end-
of-the-century celebration
Skinned corpses one by one joined the parade of the authoritarians
The celebration which began with bloodshed moved on to the feast
of flesh, chaos of scraps, an end-of-the-century disgrace
a crime, from the depths of a blooming prosperity
shouted promises to 'revitalise our great nation'

SARS is here
the virus permeates the air
At the feet of the Son of Heaven fear spreads panic and flight

清冷的皇城
让我想起十四年前的空旷和荒芜
现SARS走了
逐渐热闹起来的街市
很象遗忘了鲜血的臃肿肉体
虚幻的繁华
轻浮的希望
盛大的誓言
如同掩盖新娘哭泣的面纱
也遮住了残忍的春天
那个死于收容所的年轻大学生
是否在地下见到了十四年前的亡灵

记忆，被精致的无耻言说所切割
巧舌如簧的飞沫
从未停止过喷吐著看不见的毒汁
二百年前
林黛玉的美艳肺痨焚烧掉痴情
贾宝玉疯癫的出走如同诗的碎片
化为庄周梦蝶的翅膀，纷纷扬扬
二百年后，SARS 病毒封住了肉体之喉
政治 SARS 窒息了精神之肺
一个无法自由呼吸的民族
延续了数个世纪的高烧干咳
释放出无所不在的恐惧
纤维化的肺部
居然让死亡受得面若桃花
只能靠喝婴儿汤来乞求长寿
行为艺术家吃掉腐烂凡人尸体
与冠状病毒的飞舞争风斗艳

早已不需要赤脚行走的土地上
诗歌因没有怜悯而灭亡
那些高耸的建筑和闪亮的五彩灯光
是一块块无法融化的石头

Desolate imperial city
recalls in my mind the empty wasteland of 14 years ago
Now SARS leaves
gradually the crowds return to the market streets
as if the blood-soaked bodies have been forgotten
Illusion of prosperity
Foolish hope
The great promise is like
the veil that conceals the weeping bride
and the covered-up barbarity of that spring day
Can those young university students killed in the tents
be seen beneath earth with the dead souls of 14 years ago

Memory, severed by an eloquent depravity of speech
tongue smooth as a reed
sprays out continuous invisible venom
Two hundred years ago
the beauty Lin Daiyu, her ardour extinguished by tuberculosis
Jia Baoyu's flight of insanity like a fragment of poetry
turns into Zhuang Zhou's winged butterfly dream, fluttering on and on
Two hundred years later, the SARS virus spreads into throats
the spirit's lungs collapse from SARS politics
a nation is unable to breathe freely
On and on the centuries of burning fevers heaving coughs
ubiquitous fears released
fibrosis of the lungs
then suddenly give the dead a peach-blossom face
just drink baby soup and beg for fleshly longevity
a performance artist eats a rotting corpse
and competes with the whirling coronary virus for admiration

There's long been no need to walk the earth in bare feet
though in the absence of compassion poetry perishes
Those glowing five-colour lights built into the tallest of towers
are slab upon slab of unmeltable rock

冰冷得冻住了唯一的温暖
吸尽天下雨露的贪婪使大地龟裂
残暴浸透了沙石
一场让无耻横行无际的洗劫
宣告着人性的毁灭
而长征火箭却悠闲地探索太空的文明
还能兼职赚取国际市场的利润

那比强暴更令人绝望的罪恶
偏偏发生在青春的庭院里
一群组织严密而装备精良的土匪
肆意践踏春天的萌芽
有过人吃人的原始
有过观赏人与兽殊死角斗的野蛮
有过几百万人被推进焚尸炉的现代灭绝
人类强暴自己的姐妹
是比原子弹更具破坏力的暴行

亡灵的目光
凝视, 是为了被你凝视
倾听, 是为了被倾听
仰望在天之灵
是为了接受俯视和蔑视
被俯视, 灵魂才能被坟墓之光刺穿
谦卑之火的烧灼才能洗刷罪恶
灵魂之光会拒绝黑暗

The icy cold has frozen the final degree of warmth
greed absorbs rain and dew cracking the parched land
atrocity has seeped into the sand and stones
Let the shameless violence and boundless plunder
proclaim humanity's ruin let the Long March Rockets
seek outer-space civilisations with leisure
as one moonlights for profits in international markets

That most violent of desperate crimes
occurs in the courtyard of verdant spring
when a group of well-organised well-polished brutes
willfully trample the season's first sproutings
There have been cultures where people eat people
there have been barbarians who enjoy watching humans fight animals
there have been millions who have been forced into the incinerators
     of modern genocide
man rapes his own sisters
a more damaging atrocity than a nuclear bomb

Bright-eyed departed souls
gaze, so as to be gazed at
listen, so as to be listened to
Look up on this day of the dead
to receive their downward gaze in contempt
and thus gazed upon, the soul's light can pierce through the tomb
Only the burning flames of humility can purify guilt
for the soul's light to dispel the darkness

2004年6月4日凌晨于北京家中

十五年的黑暗
——"六·四"十五周年祭

Fifteen Years of Darkness

Before dawn at home in Beijing, 4/6/2004
Fifteenth anniversary offering for 4/6

十五年前
大屠杀在一个黎明完成
我死去并再生

十五年前
那个被刺刀染红的黎明
仍然是扎进双眼的利刃

十五年前
我的每个噩梦中都有亡灵
我看到的一切都带着血污
我写下的每一句每一笔
都是来自于坟墓的倾述

十五年了
失去自由的黑暗中
我等待这时针指向凌晨
第十五个祭日降临

今夜，在这坐没有祭坛的城市
我希望亡灵看着我的眼睛
把我的注视当作一点儿烛火
不是祭祀祖先的纸钱
不是点亮寒夜的烈焰
而是赤裸的记忆
如同不会腐烂的骨头

十五年前的此刻
广场被全副武装的戒严部队包围
反复重播的戒严令
不断转来枪声和各种血腥的消息
几个小时前
这里还人头攒动、人声鼎沸
突然熄灯的那一刻

15 years ago
a massacre took place at daybreak
I died then was reborn

15 years have passed
daybreak bayonets dyed red
is still a blade fixed in the eyes

15 years have passed
I still have nightmares of those departed souls
I see them soaked with blood
I write each stroke each line
as an outpouring of the tomb

15 years have passed
within the darkness of vanished freedom
I wait for the hour-hand to point to pre-
dawn's advent of the fifteenth anniversary offering

Tonight, in this city without altar
I hope the dead souls can see my eyes
and turn my watchful gaze into the flicker of a candle flame
Not the sacrificial spirit money for the ancestors
not the raging blaze that illuminates the cold night
but memory's nakedness
is like a bone that will not decay

15 years ago
martial-law troops besieged the Square
the military broadcast the order over and
over, a continuous transmission of gunshots and bloodthirsty news
A few hours before
the gathering crowds, the clamouring crowds
then in a blink the light was extinguished

人群的奔逃如水银泻地
留下空旷

纪念碑上的绝食棚中
我与聚集在周围的学生和市民一起
枪声不断响起
子弹撞击着纪念碑
大理石上火花四溅
我冲着刺眼的闪光灯
砸破一枝半自动步枪
但我砸不开寂静的黑夜

面对着难以预测的命运
我近乎于痴呆盯着黑暗
看不到星光的深处
是地狱还是天堂

十五年了
突然的血腥窒息了我
突然的牢狱磨砺了我

我变成一块顽石
任恐怖政治的抽打
坚硬而冰冷的表情
永远不受

从血腥的屠杀到严密的监控
那个夜晚的恐怖
从来没有离开半步
抄家过后是手铐
手铐过后是监狱
监狱过后是家门口的岗亭
贴身的跟踪
盘查来我家的客人
窃听电话

people fled like a surge of quicksilver
leaving behind an empty void

Among the hunger-strike tents on the Monument
I gathered with the students and local residents
continuous gunshots rang out
bullets struck the Monument
sparks sprayed off the marble
I released an eye-flooding flash
broke a semi-automatic rifle in half
though I can't break open the silence of the dark night

Facing an unpredictable fate
I stare dumbly into the darkness
unable to discern if the starlight abyss
is hell or paradise

15 years have passed
unexpected bloodshed has suffocated me
unexpected prisons have hardened me
I've become a thick stone
yield to the lashings of political terrors
expression hardened, frozen
always unchanged

From the massacre's bloodshed to harsh surveillance
the horrors of that night
have yet to move half-a-pace away
After the house-raid then handcuffs
after handcuffs then prison
after prison then the police sentry at my building's gate
A personal shadow
interrogates our houseguests
Phones tapped

偷窥邮箱
切断所有通信
让我变成的瞎子和聋子
与黑漆漆的夜晚
相对无言

有围墙的监狱囚禁身体
没围墙的监狱监控灵魂

十五年了
一个杀人的政权
令人绝望
一个容忍杀人政权和遗忘亡灵的民族
更令人绝望
一个大屠杀的幸存者无力为死难者讨回公道
尤其令人绝望
绝望中
记住亡灵
是唯一的希望

让黑暗变成石头
横在我记忆的荒野中

mail vetted
all forms of communication cut off
have turned me into a blind-and-deaf man
with the dark dark night
resist the silence

Walls of a cell may confine the body
but no cell walls can restrain the soul

15 years have passed
a murderer's regime
forces one to desperation
A nation that tolerates a murderous regime and forgets the killed
forces one to deeper desperation
A survivor of the massacre powerless to demand justice for the victims
forces one to the deepest desperation
But in such desperation
remembering the departed spirits
is the only hope left

Let the darkness transform into rock
across the wilderness of my memory

2005年5月18日于北京家中

记住亡灵
——"六·四"十六周年祭

Remember the Departed Souls

At home in Beijing, 18/5/2005
Sixteenth anniversary offering for 4/6

一

十六年后的夜晚
祭奠的百合变成恶梦
伤口像被撕裂的思想
结结巴巴地讲述坟墓中的故事

十六年前的那一刻
世界是羔羊
任由疯狂的宰杀
上天惊愕得无言以对
只能默默流泪或叹息

我再不能听到
响彻天空的口号和誓言
声音像个先天的聋哑人
听不到子弹的呼啸
道不出面对坦克的恐惧

我不再认识
那些年轻的面孔
饥渴的亡灵扑在母亲的胸前
却吸不出乳汁

我不再认识时间
我无法分辨昼夜
在几千年的历史中
流星找不到属于自己的墓地

1

16 years later the night's
white lily of sacrifice has transformed into nightmare
a wound like an ideal torn apart
stutter stammering through the story of the graves

16 years ago in that moment
the world was a lamb
allowing the madness of slaughter
turning to heaven speechless stupefied
weeping in silence sighing in silence

I no longer hear the sky-
echoing slogans and promises anymore
like noise to a deaf-mute
can't hear the screaming bullets
can't feel the fear of approaching tanks

I no longer recognise
those infant faces anymore
hungry and thirsty souls of the dead rush to mother's
breasts yet cannot suck one drop of milk

I no longer recognise time anymore
I can't distinguish day from night
trapped in ten thousand years of history
a falling star unable to find its own grave

二

权力、市场和灵魂的交易
血迹被金钱打扫干净
精神的毁灭
点缀着刽子手的庆典
从血腥的屠杀开始
直到人肉筵席的杯盘狼藉
诚实和尊严
母爱和怜悯
是被剥光了皮的尸体

明亮的街市和悠闲的人群
越来越精致的无耻
SARS 病毒的飞沫
弥漫在空气中
一个哮喘的民族
无法在春天里呼吸

跨世纪的罪恶和耻辱
正繁花似锦
高呼"民族复兴"的口号
高举"抵制日货"的标语
哼唱着 F4 的酷毙青春
混合着投向倭寇的石块、瓶子
突然用发嗲的童生
在秦始皇的指挥下
齐唱"连爷爷，你回来了!"

十六年前的残忍春天
披上爱国主义的时装
继续残忍

2

Power, an agreement between the market and the soul
Bloodstains washed clean with money
Spiritual devastation
decoration for the executioner's celebration
The massacre began with bloodshed
and continued with the feast of flesh, chaos of scraps
Honesty and dignity
maternal love and compassion
skinned carcasses

Glittering city streets and pleasuring crowds
grow in consummate depravity
SARS virus sprays out in droplets
spreads through the air
An asthmatic nation
cannot breathe in spring

Guilt and disgrace stretch into this century
like a flowering brocade
Shout out the slogan 'revitalise our great nation'
Lift up the sign 'boycott Japanese goods'
Hum the too cool boy-band F4
Riot, throw bottles and rocks at the 'Japanese dwarf-bandits'
Then randomly make some coy children sing
in unison at the command of the Qinshihuang president,
'Grandpa Premier Lien Chan, you've come back home!'

The cruel spring day 16 years ago
has been draped in fashionable patriotism
that perpetuates the cruelty

三

黑暗是水
没有丝毫缝隙
谎言之海
亡灵是光
即便偶尔闪亮
也能刺穿

当恐怖和遗忘同时肆虐
一群失去孩子的母亲
在颠倒的时代
执行颠倒的遗嘱
白发人带着黑发人临终的眼神
去寻找所有的坟墓
每当她们要倒下时
年轻的黑色亡灵
就会搀扶着白发人
走在泪水也被跟踪的道路上

3

The darkness is water
existing without the slightest crack
as an ocean of lies
The dead souls are light
that occasionally flares
but still pierces through

As the terror and forgetting wreak havoc
a group of mothers who've lost their children
to the insanity of the times
carry out the final testament to insanity
Seeking each grave the ones with white hair
bring the ones with black hair the eye's last glimmer
Whenever they're about to collapse
the young dead-darkened souls
hold up the white-haired mothers
to walk the road where even tears are shadowed

四

记忆黑发的亡灵
搀扶白发的母亲

锁住我的脚，我就用十指爬向你
捆住我的手，我就用膝盖和下巴爬向你
砸断我的腿，我就用断骨支撑你
勒紧我的喉，我就用窒息呼唤你
封住我的唇，我就用鼻尖亲吻你
敲掉我的牙，我就用牙床咬住你
拔光我的发，我就用秃头刺激你
挖去我的眼，我就用眼窝凝视你
腐蚀我的身，我就用气味拥抱你
碾碎我的心，我就用纤维记住你

4

Remember those black-haired dead souls
who hold up the white-haired mothers

If my feet are chained, I'll use my ten fingers to climb to you
If my hands are tied, I'll use my knees and chin to climb to you
If my legs are smashed, I'll use my broken bones to support you
If my throat's strangled, I'll use my stifled breath to call you
If my mouth's muzzled, I'll use the tip of my nose to kiss you
If my teeth are knocked out, I'll use my toothless mouth to nip you
If my hair's torn out, I'll use my bald head to nudge you
If my eyes are plucked out, I'll use my eye sockets to stare at you
If my body's eaten away, I'll use my scent to embrace you
If my heart's crushed, I'll use my nerves to remember you

2006年5月24日于北京家中

六四暗夜中的百合花
——"六·四"十七周年祭

The White Lilies in the Dark Night of June Fourth

At home in Beijing, 24/5/2006
Seventeenth anniversary offering for 4/6

已经十七年了
又是六四祭日
又是恐怖黑夜降临

一个年轻的生命
活生生的
瞬间变成枯叶
挂在初露的霞光上

感谢妻子刘霞
每年六月四日
她都会带一束白色百合回家
今年她带回十七枝百合

黑夜中的百合花
点缀着亡灵的原野
白色的百合亮着
绽开的花瓣亮着
挺拔的绿叶亮着
淡淡的花香亮着
是祭奠也是忏悔

死不瞑目的眼睛
唯一的洁白和闪亮
刺穿整个民族的精神黑暗

被禁闭在黑暗中的百合花
是亡灵之光
打开我的灵魂
看见母亲们
看见维多利亚公园里
看到世界各地
为亡灵们点燃的烛火

It's been 17 years
and once more June Fourth approaches
once more the terrifying dark night descends

A life
so young so alive
in an instant becomes a dried leaf
suspended in the sun's first light

I thank my wife Liu Xia
for bringing home a bouquet of white lilies
each year on the 4th day of the 6th month
this year she's brought 17 flowering-stems home

The white lilies in the dark night
stitch the open fields of the departed spirits
The whiteness of the lilies luminous
the bursting petals luminous
the upright green leaves luminous
the faint faint fragrance luminous
a memorial offering a penance

Eyes that cannot shut in death
the only gleam of purity
pierces the nation's spiritual darkness

The white lilies locked in the darkness
are the light of the departed spirits
Open up my soul
to see their mothers
to see Victoria Park
to see each place in the world
with candles blazing for the dead souls

在失去自由的日子里
百合花陷入黑暗
犹如时间与亡灵们对话
洁白　为亡灵点燃的祈祷之火
凝视、灼热并照亮我面对绝对空无

僵硬的表情
被尘土抹去的歌声
以及再次开花的眼睛
面对野蛮的劫掠
有一种坚韧
巍然不动
如同荒芜的土地
开满了金黄色的向日葵
那精神失常的凡高
播种太阳的凡高
用飞翔的耳朵倾听色彩的凡高
战胜过地狱和天堂的凡高

恶毒的觉醒
充溢在绝望的每一时刻
黑夜倒悬
百合开放得朦胧
无言的春天落花
把我从深渊中托起

As the day loses its freedom
the white lilies submerged in the darkness
are a dialogue between time and the dead
the purity   the flames of prayer that burn for the departed spirits
stare out   scorch and illuminate the utter void I face

Hardened expressions
dust drowns the singing and the eyes
blooming open once again
To face the savage plunder
requires an enduring tenacity
an unmoving brilliance
as if across the desolate wilderness
a riot of golden sunflowers blossomed
deranged Van Gogh
sun-sowing Van Gogh
flying-ear-listening-to-colours Van Gogh
persevering-through-hell-and-heaven Van Gogh

Bitter awakening
permeates each moment of desperation
suspended in the dark night
white-lily bloom an obscure haze
the fallen flowers of silent spring
lift me out of the abyss

2007年6月2日于北京家中

那个春天的亡灵
——"六·四"十八周年祭

The Dead Souls of Spring

At home in Beijing, 2/6/2007
Eighteenth anniversary offering for 4/6

在春天，感受大雪
被监控的目光
感受今夜的亡灵
雪花是否飘进坟墓？
是否把我的雪中之梦带去？
纪念碑的斜影
把恐怖之夜投进我的瞳孔

那个春天，被刺刀惊吓
突然面目狰狞
孕育生命季节
呕出巨大的坟墓
曾经温暖的阳光
结成阴沟里的冰
浸满了血污的泪滴
如同沙尘暴中的飞雪

那个春天，扑到在坦克的履带下
纵使我掏出全部智慧和献上赤裸的灵魂
也达不到坟墓的高度

那个春天，梦想变成母亲们终生的痛
之后的每个春天
都被锁链捆绑
但我知道
那是亡灵留下的遗产和考验

那个春天，我希望崩溃
让我单薄的身体和懦弱的灵魂
先于第一束阳光而离去
害怕任何英雄式的壮举
又无力进行自我亵渎
封闭的生命
在空无中挣扎
只能点燃一支烟

In spring, feel the heavy snows
Eyes under surveillance
feel the night's dead souls
Can snowflakes drift into the tomb?
Can my snowed-in dreams be taken, too?
The Monument's towering shadow
casts the night's terrors into my dilated eyes

That spring day, petrified by bayonets
the sudden ferocity of faces
Life's pregnant season
regurgitates the tomb's immensity
Sunlight once so warm
gutter water surges
with blood-soaked tears
snow-swirl in a sandstorm

That spring day, felled beneath tank treads
Even if I could offer my naked soul in full knowingness
it won't reach the heights of the tomb

That spring day, the dream turned into a lifelong ache
for the mothers, each spring after
has been bound in shackles
though I know
the departed souls have left us a legacy and a test

That spring day, my hopes crumbled
as my weakened body and cowering soul
left before sun's first light
Too scared for heroic feats
no strength for self-profanities
Sealed up life
struggles in the empty void
Just light a cigarette

紧紧抓住每一个堕落的瞬间
活下去是一种考验
谁也不知到
不一个小时会不会崩溃?

我吧一面镜子漆成黑色
在用舌头把它舔得光可鉴人
重新复活的眼睛望着我
看到的将是什么?
让一条狗满意
一块骨头是不够的
让零从一开始
动动手已经足矣
有人每天活在反抗中
也都有人死于恐惧
信仰的炸弹四处开花
把自己雕刻在一块石头上
然后沉入海底
永不干枯的记忆
做一个虚无着
像王维或陶渊明那样在小河边写诗
乞讨杯中物
权作潇洒的见证
以某种方式结束痛苦
埋葬纪念碑的慷慨

亡灵之光
穿越高墙和铁条
流入我的体内
融化深涧里的顽石
坚硬的棱角一点点圆润
自恋的人多么脆弱、渺小、狂躁
即便伟大的时刻近在眼前
也无力承受

and grasp tight each moment of depravity
for survival is a test
Who doesn't know
whether or not the next hour will crumble?

I paint the surface of a mirror black
and use my tongue to lick the bright reflection
Newly revived eyes stare back at me
what do they see?
For a dog to be satisfied
a single bone isn't enough
To start over from zero
a wave of the hands is enough
There are people who live a life of resistance each day
and there are people everywhere who die from fear
Bombs of conviction bloom in the four directions
carve the self into stone
that then sinks to the sea-bottom
never-fading memory
Become a nihilist and pretend
to be Wang Wei or Tao Yuanming writing verse by a little stream
Beg for cups of wine
assume the right to be a free and unrestrained witness
as a way to end suffering
to bury the Monument's ferocity

The light of the departed souls
crosses a high wall through iron bars
flows into my body
melts the unfeeling rock deep within me
hard-edged corners slowly turn smooth and soft
How fragile the narcissist, how tiny and impetuous
even if an enormous moment rises before his eyes
he has no will to bear it

从内心中取走那束仅有的余光吧
为我照亮一条路

如同向海展示天
向天展示海
向我的灵魂展示你的灵魂

亡灵的春天守候我
胜过海涛对岩石的拍打
每年每月每天每时每刻
总有一天
岩石会感动、会流泪、会崩裂
然后注入大海

我说不清
是亡灵让那个残忍的春天升华
还是那个残忍得春天让亡灵升华
如果我是一枝烟
就用燃烧兑现诺言
如果我烧完
就用灰烬兑现诺言

To take the heart's lone glowing ray
and illuminate the way for me

As facing the sea reveals the sky
and facing the sky reveals the sea
facing my soul reveals your soul

The dead souls of spring wait for me
to surpass the waves crashing against rock
Each year each month each day each hour each moment
inevitably there'll be a day
when rock will be moved, weep, and burst apart
then fuse with the sea's vastness

I can't say for sure
if it's the dead souls sublimating that cruel spring
or that cruel spring sublimating the dead souls
If I'm just a cigarette
then use the burning embers to keep the promise
If I burn out
then use the ashes to keep the promise

2008年5月

孩子·母亲·春天
——"六·四"十九周年祭

Child – Mother – Spring

5/2008
Nineteenth anniversary offering for 4/6

一

十九年前
残忍的六月突降
风很冷
雨水垒满碎石
砸在母亲的心头
春天的残忍
没有萌芽便凋零
没有花朵便腐烂
在一切还未到来之前
一切已经被彻底毁灭

凝视年轻的遗像
一根针插进母亲的眼睛
瞬间的失明
大脑的雪亮
泪水像枯草
萧瑟在荒野中
遥远的亡灵
那么遥远
夜倒悬
旗帜被抛向水中
波纹扭曲的影子
顷刻笼罩大地

19 years ago
June's cruel tragedy
Wind so cold
rain flooded piles of broken stone
poured into the hearts of the Mothers
Cruel June
without shoots it withers
without flowers it fades
Before everything not-yet arrived
everything was wholly destroyed

Staring at his funeral portrait so young
a needle pierces the Mother's eye
Flash of blindness
Brain's snowbrightness
Tears like the soughs
of dried grass in the wilderness
Departed souls faraway
so faraway
Fallen night suspended
Flag flung into water
ripple twisted shadows
soon enshroud the land

二

出门前，孩子曾许诺
为母亲画出六月的风
温暖的绿色的风
追风的孩子突然倒下
后脑中弹
右手瘫痪
画笔被钢铁碾碎
六月的风变成血色
灌满母亲的身体

有人说
为自由而死
是一种伟大
为自由殉难的孩子
已经接近神圣
而母爱，基于血缘
宁愿自己的孩子
活在平凡中
如今，浪漫的年龄远去
留下生命废墟的记忆
十九年了
每一年都是三百六十五呼唤
回来吧
扑倒在春天的孩子
映在母亲的眼底

没有鲜花和青草的坟墓
有白发缠绕
每个夜晚
亡灵都能触摸到了母亲的天空
像十月怀胎
倾听母亲的心跳

2

Before leaving home, the child promised
to draw June's wind for Mother
the green warmth of wind
Then the wind-chasing child suddenly collapsed
with a bullet in the back of his head
left hand paralysed
paintbrush crushed by steel
June's wind turned the colour of blood
filling Mother's body

Some say
to die for freedom
is a kind of greatness
that a child sacrificed for freedom
attains the sacred
but maternal love, rooted in ties of blood
prefers its own child
to live an ordinary life
Now, the age of romance is long gone
what life left the ruins of memory
19 years have passed
each year 365 cries
for their return
fallen children of spring
reflected in the eyes of the Mothers

Graves with no flowers nor greenness of grass
as white hair twists down
night after night
the dead souls can touch Mother's emptiness
as if in the tenth month of pregnancy
listening for Mother's heartbeat

三

亡灵的春天弥漫一切
春天的亡灵穿透一切
死亡唤起的觉醒
挽救了母亲绝望的时刻
不抱怨彼岸的遥远
不蔑视此岸的平庸
生命无价
甚至连蚂蚁
也不容贬低
谁的眼泪
能穿越深涧里的顽石
让坚硬的棱角一点点圆润
从还有温度的身体
释放出那束仅有的余光
为母亲照亮一条路
屠杀升华了亡灵
亡灵升华母爱
超越血缘
超越高悬于头上的太阳

3

The spring of the departed spirits permeates everything
The departed spirits of spring pierce everything
The wakening call of the dead
saves the Mothers from desperation
Do not complain about the distance of the other shore
Do not despise the indifference of this shore
Life is priceless
even to an ant
it also cannot tolerate disparagement
Whose tears
can pass through the unfeeling rock deep within
to melt hard-edged corners smooth
with what warmth's still left in the body
release the heart's lone glowing ray
to illuminate the way for the Mothers
The massacre has sublimated the departed spirits
the departed spirits have sublimated the Mothers' love
transcends the ties of blood
transcends the sun suspended high above

四

逃避自由的人活着
灵魂却死于恐惧中
渴望自由的人死去
亡灵却活在反抗中
突然撕裂的思想
看不见疤痕的伤口
压抑太久的声音
讲述坟墓的故事
伤痕累累的烛火
洞彻灵魂的荒芜
亡灵的目光
凝视着母亲
母亲的目光
逼视每一个春天
母亲对六月许下的诺言
让影子叹息
让石头飞翔

4

Those who flee freedom live on
but their souls die in fear
Those who thirst for freedom die
but their souls live on in resistance
An ideal abruptly torn apart
unable to see the wound's scar
Voices suppressed for too long
tell the story of the tomb
wound after candle-flame wound
with clarity perceives the soul's desolation
The gaze of the departed spirits
fixed on the Mothers
the gaze of the Mothers
forced to see each spring
Mothers facing the promise of June
to let shadows sigh
to let rocks fly

五

年轻的亡灵
不要说失败
不要说荒废了十九年时光
在母亲的祭奠中
孩子们倒下的那一刻
已经永恒
曾经的热血
至今依然沸腾
割不断的烛光和夜晚
超越年龄
也超越死亡
把未完成的爱
交给母亲的白发
年轻的亡灵
相信母亲吧
母爱是火
即便熄灭了
也会用灰烬兑现诺言

5

Young departed souls
do not say defeat
do not say 19 years of light's been wasted
in the eulogies of the Mothers
The children who collapsed in that moment
have passed into everlastingness
Blood once warm
to this day still boiling
The candle flames cannot be cut off from the night
Age transcendent
Death transcendent
Offer unfinished love
for the white hair of the Mothers
Young departed souls
believe in the Mothers
for maternal love is fire
which even if extinguished
can use its ashes to keep the promise

2009年5月18日于北京家中

我身体中的六四

——"六·四"二十周年祭

June Fourth in My Body

At home in Beijing, 18/5/2009
Twentieth anniversary offering for 4/6

这个日子
似乎越来越遥远
但它之于我
是一根留在身体中的针
是一群失去了孩子的母亲
在缝补残梦时遗忘的
它一直在寻找一双手
接替母亲们的工作

这根针
寻遍了我的全身
常常游弋到心脏的边缘
仔细倾听心的跳动
偶尔
用针尖试探地触碰心的表面
刺死过无数幼稚的冲动和欲望

这根针
曾长久地停留在心脏的边缘
下决心奋力一刺
结束所有的罪恶
行动前的瞬间
它犹豫了
不敢继续向前
它知道生命的脆弱
抵不住轻轻地一扎
应该留下一点余地, 一点时间
让血液把锈迹全部吸收

这根针
仅仅是由于
没有找到那双手
它才踌躇

The day
seems more and more distant
and yet for me it
remains a needle inside my body
remains a crowd of Mothers who've lost their children
mending the cruel dream's time of forgetting
It continues to seek willing hands
to take over the work of the Mothers

This needle
searches inside my body
often circles the heart's periphery
cautiously listens to the pulse-beat
sometimes
uses its tip to probe the heart's surface
and kills off the many naive, impulsive desires

This needle
that has stayed for so long round the heart's periphery
is determined to plunge inside
and bring an end to all guilt
but then just before acting
it hesitates
not daring to move forward
It knows of life's frailty
can't resist giving a light prick
should leave a little space, a little time
for the flow of blood to absorb rust-traces

This needle
only because willing
hands have not yet been found
falters, wavers

针的本性很野蛮
渴望穿透一切
以血来喂养其锋芒
它的锈迹渗入血液
血液的流动使皮肤发紫发青

这根针
留在身体中
只为了一个简单的理由
寻找一只手
以确立它的永恒道义性
它不允许懦弱的神经肆虐地颤抖
针尖成为良知的守望者

命运把我交给了它
死于这根针是早晚的事
犹如冬日把一滴水交给冰
或夏天把一只眼睛交给炽热的太阳
现在，此刻
我正在感受它的锋芒和锐利
锋芒照亮内脏
锐利的滑动清洗懦弱

这根针
已经习惯了我睡眠中的胡思乱想和梦中呓语
昨夜惊醒时
听到它发出清脆的声响
闪光而奇妙
像身体中的一道彩虹
阴云密布的天空中
它的生命比我的文字更长久
它充满活力
悠然地游曳在身体中
每一次无意中的触碰

The needle's savage nature
thirsts to puncture everything
Blood nourishes its point
its rust-traces enter the bloodstream
circulate, bruise the skin blue bruise purple

This needle
stays in the body
for the simple reason
of seeking the hands
that would establish its permanent moral nature
It doesn't permit spineless nerves to spread waves of trembling
The needle tip turns into the watchman of conscience

Fate has given me to it
to die by this needle is a matter of inevitability
as winter gives a water-drop to ice
or summer gives an eye to the blazing sun
Now, at this moment
I can feel the sharpness of its point
a point that illuminates the inner organs
a sliding sharpness that purges spinelessness

This needle
has adapted to my sleep's wild imaginings and dream-state ravings
Last night woke
up to its metallic murmur
a flashing brilliance
as if a rainbow in the body
in a sky thick with dark clouds
Its life lasts longer than my written words
it overflows with vitality
leisurely trawls through the body
Each of its inadvertent touches

使它更闪亮更尖锐
更有不可动摇的合法性

在我的身体中
有一个死角格外荒凉
这根针
使尸体发出呻吟
使睁不开的双眼在黑夜里目光如注
透视出一切
膨胀的罪恶不安于角落的狭窄
要深入到记忆的核心
那些背叛的时刻
为正义蒙上虚假的激动
我的灵魂与心脏分离
如同一个淫棍的肮脏生殖器
玷污了那个纯粹的夜晚

真冷呀
针，盲目地游走
足以使血液结成冰
被亵渎的死亡
如同被抢劫一空的陵园
大理石墓碑前的烛火跃入眼底
能熔化这根针吗?
身体中的针尖能变成烛火
温暖每一块墓碑下的夜晚吗?
我等待那只手
以缝补残梦的果决和耐心
让这根针刺穿心脏
肉体的悲哀和神经的哭号
毒化了思想
升华了诗

intensifies its brilliance its stabbing point
its unswayed legitimacy

Inside my body
there's a most desolate dead corner
This needle
that makes the corpses groan
injects eyes forced shut in the dark night with a visionary light
Sight penetrates everything
Swollen guilt distressed in the cramped corner
wants to sink into the core of memory
that moment of betrayal
concealing justice in a pretence of excitement
My soul separates from the heart
as if a philanderer's diseased genitals
have defiled the purity of night

Such a cold
needle, wandering blind
causes blood to congeal into ice
The denounced dead
are a looted cemetery
Gravestone candle flames leap into the eyes
Can the needle be melted?
Can the needle tip turn into a flame inside the body
and warm each gravestone of the night?
I wait for those willing hands
to stitch the cruel dream with resolute patience
and let the needle pierce into the heart's chambers
body's flesh sorrow nerves cry out
Poisoned ideal
sublimated poetry

Five Poems for Liu Xia

早晨

在灰色的高墙
和一阵剁菜声之间
早晨被捆束被切割
被一种灵魂的瘫软所消融

不知道光与黑暗的区别
怎样透过我的瞳孔呈现
坐在锈迹中我无法确定
是狱中的镣铐之光
还是墙外的自然之神
白昼的背叛令骄傲的太阳
惊愕不已

这个早晨徒劳地广阔
你在远方
将爱的夜晚珍藏

30/6/1997

Daybreak

Over the tall ashen wall, between
the sound of vegetables being chopped
daybreak is bound and severed
dissipated by a paralysis of spirit

What is the difference
between the light and the darkness
that seems to surface through my eyes'
apertures, from my seat of rust
I can't tell if it's the glint of chains
in the cell, or the god of nature
behind the wall
The day's dissidence
makes the arrogant
sun stunned to no end

Daybreak a vast emptiness
you in a far place
with nights of love stored away

30/6/1997

狱中的小耗子

一只小耗子爬过铁条
在窗台上来回走动
剥落的墙在看它
吸饱了血的蚊子在看它
它也吸引了天上的月亮
银色的投影似乎在飞
一种罕见的美

今晚的耗子很绅士
不吃不喝不磨牙
瞪着那双贼亮的眼睛
在月光下散步

26/5/1999

A Small Rat in Prison

A small rat passes through the iron bars
paces back and forth on the window ledge
the peeling walls are watching him
the blood-filled mosquitoes are watching him
he even draws the moon from the sky, silver
shadow casts down
a rare beauty, as if in flight

A very gentryman the mouse tonight
doesn't eat nor drink nor grind his teeth
as he stares with his sly bright eyes
strolling in the moonlight

26/5/1999

贪婪的囚犯

一个囚犯
挤占了你的生活
如此贪婪而凶残
竟不允许你为自己
买一束花一块巧克力
一件漂亮的时装
他不给你时间
一分钟都不给

他把你当作手中的烟
吸的干干净净
连灰烬也不属于你自己
他身在共产党的监狱
为你建造了灵魂的牢房
没有门没有窗
没有一线缝隙
把你锁在孤独中
直到霉烂

他逼你在尸体的控诉中
忍受每一个夜晚
他控制着你的笔
让你不停地写信
让你绝望地寻找希望
你的痛苦被践踏成
他无聊中的唯一乐趣

你的那只鸟
迷失在他手掌的
复杂纹路中
被四条掌纹缠绕
其中的每一条
都欺骗过你

Greed's Prisoner

A prisoner
presses into the crowd of your life
so cruel and full of greed
won't even let you
buy a bouquet of flowers for yourself
a piece of chocolate, a pretty dress
He doesn't give you
time, not a single minute
does he give you

The cigarettes in your hand
he smokes and smokes so neatly
Even the ashes don't belong to you, his body
in the prison of the Communist Party
so that the spirit-cell built for you
without a door without a window
without a thread of a crack
locks you in solitude
until you rot

He forces you to endure each night
in the corpse of denunciation
He controls your pen
makes you write endless letters
makes you desperate to find hope
your suffering's been trampled into
his boredom's one pleasure

That bird of yours
is lost in the torturous palm-
lines of his hand
where each path
has betrayed you

这个目无一切的独裁者
劫掠了你的尸体
一夜之间白发覆顶
造就了他的传奇和神话
当他自以为功德圆满时
你已经一无所有
可这囚犯仍然
死死地抓住你空白的未来

又到日子了
他又发布命令
你又该独自上路
没有身体没有记忆
用被掏空的生命
背着带给他的
沉重书籍上路
他很善于投机
从不放过
每一次剥夺你的机会

亲爱的
我的妻子
在这尘世的
所有卑鄙之中
你为什么
单单挑选我来忍受

23/7/1999

This emptied-eyed all-ignorant dictatorship
has plundered your corpse
in one night white hair covers the crown
completing his legend, his myth
the moment he sees himself brimming with righteous deeds
you already possess nothing
but this prisoner
has deathly-seized the blank space of your future

Another day arrives
once more he issues an order
once more you must walk the road alone
without body without memory
using this hollowed life
to carry his heavy book-load
on the road to him
He is very good at exploiting
each chance to dispossess you
of your possibilities

Beloved
my wife
in this dust-weary world of
so much depravity
why do you
choose me alone to endure

23/7/1999

渴望逃离

抛开虚拟的殉难
我渴望躺在你的脚下
这是除了与死亡纠缠的
唯一义务
也是心如明镜时
持久的幸福

你的脚趾不会折断
一只猫紧跟在身后
真想替你赶走它
它转过头
向我伸出利爪
蓝眼睛的深处
似乎有一座监狱
如果我盲目跨出
哪怕仅仅一步
就会变成一条鱼

12/8/1999

Longing to Escape

Abandoning the imagined martyrdom
I long to lie at your feet, besides
being tied to death this is
my one duty
when the heart's mirror-
clear, an enduring happiness

Your toes will not break
a cat closes in behind
you, I want to shoo him away
as he turns his head, extends
a sharp claw toward me
Deep within his blue eyes
there seems to be a prison
if I blindly step out
of with even the slightest step
I'd turn into a fish

12/8/1999

一封信就够了

一封信就够了
我就能超越一切
向你说话

当风吹过
夜晚用自己的血
写出一个隐秘的词
让我记住
每一个字都是最后一个字

你身体中的冰
融化成火的神话
刽子手的目光中
愤怒变成石头

两条铁轨突然重叠
扑向灯光的飞蛾
以永恒的姿态
跟随你的影子

1/8/2000

One Letter Is Enough

One letter is enough
for me to transcend everything and face
you to speak

As the wind blows past
the night
uses its own blood
to write a secret verse
that reminds me each
word is the last word

The ice in your body
melts into a myth of fire
in the eyes of the executioner
fury turns to stone

Two sets of iron rails
unexpectedly overlap
A moth flaps toward lamp
light, an eternal gesture
traces your shadow

1/8/2000

Notes

Dedication

Tiananmen Mothers: Activist group that started as a one-woman campaign initiated by Professor Ding Zilin whose son was shot by government troops during June Fourth. The organisation seeks a government apology and reparations for the victims of the massacre. See Liu Xiaobo's introduction.

Introduction

Part 1
Lu Xun (1881–1936): Pioneering author of modernist China and central figure of the May Fourth Movement. Translator of Nikolai Gogol, Alexander Fadayev, Kuriyagawa Hakuson, Anatoly Lunacharsky, among others.

Part 2
Madame Snow: Lois Wheeler Snow, wife of journalist Edgar Snow, who returned to Beijing with her son in the year 2000 to meet Ding Zilin and support the Tiananmen Mothers. The Chinese government prevented the meeting.

little comforts: *xiao kang*, a Confucian term in the *Classic of Rites* that refers to an ideal society of relative prosperity which would eventually lead to *da tong*, or 'universal harmony'. Deng Xiaoping and Jiang Zemin both revived the concept of a *xiao kang* society to describe modernisation and an expanding middle class of moderate economic, materialistic well-being. Often translated as 'moderate prosperity' or 'well-off'. See poem 5 of the sixth anniversary offering, poem 3 of the seventh anniversary offering, and the thirteenth anniversary offering.

Yu Qiuyu: b. 1946. Popular Shanghai-rooted cultural critic. *A Bitter Journey through Culture* (1992) is his most famous work, though none of his books has been published in English yet.

Wang Shuo: b. 1958. Popular novelist and screenwriter and life resident of Beijing. Driving force of 'hooligan literature' during the late 1980s and 1990s. Author of *Please Don't Call Me Human* (1989) and *Playing for Thrills* (1989).

Liu Sola: b. 1955. Writer, musician, and composer. Author of the novellas *You Have No Other Choice* (1985) and *Blue Sky Green Sea* (1985), and the novel *Chaos and All That* (1991). Her album *Blues in the East* (1994) was produced by Bill Laswell and features jazz legend Henry Threadgill, Umar Bin Hassan of the Last Poets, the pipa player Wu Man, guitarist James Blood Ulmer of the Music Revelation Ensemble, Parliament/Funkadelic drummer Jerome Bailey, bassist Fernando Saunders, violinist Jason Hwang, Ned Rothenberg and Ralph Samuelson on shakuhachi, percussionists Aiyb Dieng and Yukio Tsuji, and organist Amina Claudine Myers of the Liberation Music Orchestra. How this stellar conjunction of musicians occurred on Liu Sola's US debut is one of eight million stories in the naked city.

Liao Yiwu: b. 1958. Arrested in 1990 for making a recording of his poem *Requiem*, and for making a film with five other poets, *The Massacre*, which commemorated the victims of June Fourth. Imprisoned for four years; the other five poets were released in February 1992. Recent books in English include *The Corpse Walker: Real Life Stories: China from the Bottom Up* and *God Is Red: The Secret Story of How Christianity Survived and Flourished in Communist China*.

Miss Liu Hezhen: A student killed in the 18 March Massacre in 1926. See afterword.

Part 4
Yu the Great ... passing his home three times: A legendary story of Yu the Great, the sage-king founder of the Xia Dynasty (ca. 2070–1600 BC). The story is recorded in the *Lienü Zhuan* (*Biographies of Exemplary Women*) compiled by Han Dynasty scholar Liu Xiang ca. 18 BC.

Jin Yuelin (1895–1984): Prominent Chinese philosopher who lived next door to his friends, the married architects Lin Huiyin and Liang Sicheng. Jin Yuelin remained single his whole life due to his love for Lin Huiyin. Liang Sicheng was the chief architect of the Monument to the People's Heroes, which Lin Huiyin also helped design.

First Anniversary Offering

Part 1
Monument waves of weeping: Monument to the People's Heroes completed in 1958. The front of the ten-storey obelisk is engraved with Mao's words: 'Eternal glory to the people's heroes'; ten white marble bas-reliefs in the lower plinth narrate China's revolutionary history since 1840. The monument stands in the centre of Tiananmen Square and its site served as centre of the June Fourth protests following the death of ousted General Secretary Hu Yaobang.

Sixth Anniversary Offering

Part 3
Goddess of Democracy: Statue designed by student protesters during June Fourth and raised in the Square in the early morning of May 30. The Party denounced the statue in the press, saying, 'The Square is sacred. No one has the power to add any permanent memorial or to remove anything from the Square.' On 3 June the statue was destroyed by a tank, which also crushed some protestors. See afterword.

Seventh Anniversary Offering

Part 3

Jiang Zemin: b. 1926. General Secretary of the Communist Party from 1989 to 2002; President of the People's Republic of China from 1993 to 2003; Chairman of the Central Military Commission from 1989 to 2004.

Zhongnanhai: 'Central and southern seas': refers to the central headquarters for the Communist Party and the State Council in central Beijing, next to the Forbidden City.

Passing away as the river passes: See the *Analects of Confucius,* Volume 16, Chapter 9.

Part 4

Li Peng: Fourth premier of the People's Republic of China from 1987 to 1998, and the Chairman of the Standing Committee of the National People's Congress from 1998 to 2003. Before that he was an electrical engineer, and later served as vice-minister and minister of the electricity and water industries. His youngest son, Li Xiaoyong, was accused of masterminding a $60 million futures-trading scam and escaped to Hong Kong under a false name, eventually settling in Singapore. His eldest son, Li Xiaopeng, and his daughter, Li Xiaolin, have made a fortune in the energy sector in China.

Chang'an Avenue: 'Eternal Peace Avenue', an enormous ten-lane road that passes between the gate and square of Tiananmen. Most of Beijing's monuments are located along this road, which defines the city's east–west axis.

prostitutes: Until 2002, the possession of a condom by a female worker in a nightclub constituted evidence of prostitution in the Chinese legal system and could be used as grounds for prosecution.

Eighth Anniversary Offering

Nüwa: In Chinese mythology, a goddess of fertility with the body of a snake who created humans and repaired the wall of Heaven. Her husband Fu Xi, the first of the mythic Three Sovereigns of ancient China, was also her brother.

Jingwei: Daughter of the Yan Emperor who perished in the East Sea. Upon her death she transformed into a bird determined to fill the sea up with rocks and sticks as revenge.

Tan Sitong (1865–1898): Philosopher, poet, and revolutionary of the late Qing Dynasty. On the order of Empress Dowager Ci Xi, he and five others were beheaded on 28 September, 1898, before thousands of onlookers for his involvement in the Hundred Days' Reform. Tan was part of a 'new poetry revolution' with the poets Huang Zunxian, Xia Zengyou, and Liang Qichao. Liang once wrote: 'Those who want to be a Columbus or Magellan of the poetic realm must follow three principles: first, a new world of perceptions; second, new vocabularies; third, incorporating the two in the style of the ancients.' Tan Sitong is the author of A *Philosophy of Humanity* and *Poems from the Misty Room* (note 'misty' here can also be translated as 'verdant' or 'lush' or 'hazy' and is not the same 'misty' as the prominent post-Cultural Revolution Misty School of poetry, which can also be translated as the Obscure School).

Ah Q: Self-delusional protagonist in Lu Xun's short story 'The True Story of Ah Q'.

Qin Shi Huang's Tomb: Qin Shi Huang was the ruler of Qin from 246 BC to 221 BC during the Warring States Period, and the first emperor of a unified China. He's infamous for initiating the building of the Great Wall and a burning of books so that his reign could not be compared with past dynasties. Many scholars were also burned for owning forbidden books. The vast Terracotta Army in Xi'an was buried with the Emperor so that he could rule another empire in the afterlife. More than six hundred tombs of slaves, servants, labourers, concubines, and scholars buried alive with the Emperor have been discovered. This city-structured burial ground was discovered by local farmers in 1974, and though the main tomb of the Emperor has been located, it hasn't been excavated yet. See poem 3 of the tenth anniversary offering and poem 2 of the sixteenth anniversary offering.

Xi Shi: One of the legendary Four Beauties of ancient China.

Lin Daiyu: Protagonist of Cao Xueqin's novel *Dream of the Red Chamber* written in the eighteenth century and considered one of China's Four Great Classical Novels. Lin Daiyu and Jia Baoyu are portrayed as star-crossed lovers during feudal times. They also appear in the fourteenth anniversary offering, 'Beneath the Gaze of the Departed Souls'.

AIDS: From the time of the first reported cases of AIDS in 1985 to 2002, the Chinese government's response to the spread of the virus was characterised by official denial and inaction. It was considered to be only a male homosexual disease (as it was in the US during the 1980s) and a disease of 'the West', thus it became known as *aizibing*: 'the loving capitalism disease'.

Guo Moruo (1892–1978): Prominent poet, historian, archaeologist, and translator of Upton Sinclair, Goethe, Shelley, Tolstoy, Nietzsche, H. G. Wells, and others. Like Lu Xun he studied medicine in Japan and then abandoned it for literature. His most famous book of poems, *Goddesses* (1921), carries the spirits of Qu Yuan, Kabir, and Tagore.

Ninth Anniversary Offering

Richie Ren's 'Too Softhearted': The translator experienced firsthand the painful spread of this sappy pop tune through the interstices of the land.

Tenth Anniversary Offering

Part 4

Liu Bang: Personal name of Emperor Gao, first ruler of the Han Dynasty (206 BC–220 AD), whose mother is said to have been impregnated by a dragon.

Chang Ling Tomb: The largest of the thirteen Ming Dynasty Tombs where the Yongle Emperor (Zhu Di, 1360–1420) and Empress Xushi are buried. Construction began in 1409 and was completed in 1427. The Emperor also initiated construction of the Forbidden City in 1406.

Mausoleum: Chairman Mao Memorial Hall, one of the five monuments in Tiananmen Square. It was completed in 1977, and displays Mao's mummified body in a crystal coffin. Also appears in the thirteenth anniversary offering.

Eleventh Anniversary Offering

Su Bingxian: Mother of twenty-one-year-old Zhao Long, a demonstrator during the June Fourth Movement who was found shot three times in the chest.

Thirteenth Anniversary Offering

Thirteen Tombs: The thirteen Ming Dynasty Tombs in Beijing. See note for Chang Ling Tomb above.

Three Represents: Flimsy ideology proposed by General Secretary Jiang Zemin who added it to the PRC Constitution as well as the CCP Constitution. To generalise the generalised theory: to represent the development needs of productivity, to represent the advance of culture, to represent the fundamental interests of the people.

Fourteenth Anniversary Offering

SARS: Severe acute respiratory syndrome caused by the SARS coronavirus. First broke out in Guangdong Province in November 2002. Like AIDS, China initially denied the emerging epidemic. Eventually in 2003, the crisis forced the government to significantly change their SARS policy, which also lead to significant HIV/AIDS policy reform.

Sixteenth Anniversary Offering

Part 2

Lien Chan: Premier of Taiwan from 1993 to 1997, Vice President of Taiwan from 1996 to 2000, and the Chairman of the Guomindang from 2000 to 2005. He received the inaugural Confucius Peace Prize in December 2010, an official prize endorsed by the Chinese government in response to the awarding of the Nobel Peace Prize to Liu Xiaobo.

Seventeenth Anniversary Offering

Victoria Park: Public park in Hong Kong and, since 1990, the site of an annual candlelight vigil in commemoration of those killed during June Fourth.

Eighteenth Anniversary Offering

Wang Wei (699–759): Treasured poet, painter, calligrapher, musician, and devout Buddhist of the Tang Dynasty.

Tao Yuanming (365–427): Tao Qian, revered Daoist-Confucian Jin Dynasty poet; worked for the government as a military adviser and magistrate, then left and became a farmer for twenty-some years.

Twentieth Anniversary Offering

At home in Beijing, 18/5/2009: The date and place of composition for this elegy is questionable. Liu Xiaobo was detained by the Chinese authorities on 8 December, 2008, and held 'at an undisclosed location in Beijing' until his formal arrest in June 2009. It is possible that Liu Xiaobo wrote this elegy at the end of 2008 and projected a time and place in keeping with the spirit of the book (and perhaps a desire to be home). Liu Xia posted a video of herself in June 2010 reading a twenty-first anniversary offering of Liu Xiaobo's that was actually the fifteenth elegy. In the video, Liu Xia says that he has been in prison 'without paper or pen and cannot write poetry anymore'. Why the nineteenth anniversary elegy bears no place of composition at all is also a mystery.

Translator's Afterword

Around the spring of each year for twenty years Liu Xiaobo has been writing his *June Fourth Elegies*, a book divided into twenty sections, each section of which consists of a poem or series of poems written as a memorial offering to those killed in the 1989 Tiananmen Massacre. At the beginning of each elegy the place of composition is noted (at home, in a re-education camp, under house arrest, in a bar) along with the title and the date of completion. Poets in the Persian and Arabic *marthiya* tradition have been elegising the sacrifice of Muhammad's grandson Husayn ibn 'Alī in the Battle of Krabala since the seventh century, but has there ever been such a lifework of elegiac remembrance in verse as Liu Xiaobo's? A work so tortuously compelled by experienced history and individual circumstance, by such deep mourning, guilt, regret, and the hope for justice and redemption, written year after year? This volume collects two decades of anniversary offerings from 1990 to 2009: offerings to the dead, to a failed revolution, to murdered innocents, to the forgotten. It is an open-ended work that is neither monumental gesture nor sealed epitaph but scorched by the actual, soaked in spilt blood, shadowed by disaster's memory, awaiting the dead souls' flight from the tomb. Of such poetry it is profoundly apparent how impossible it is to contrive the live sparks of experience through which an aesthetic arises.

Elegy seeks the immortality of the who or what being elegised; in a negative sense it is a refutation of meaninglessness and transience.

Our conception of elegy veers to the Greeks, to Callimachus and Theocritus, and on to Propertius and Virgil's pastoral, perhaps leaps to Goethe's *Roman Elegies*, Milton's 'Lycidas', Rilke's *Duino Elegies*, and to Muriel Rukeyser's 'We tell beginnings . . .'. Or Jeremiah's *Lamentations*, Rumi's *Divan-e Shams*, Lorca's *Llanto*, passages of Robert Duncan's *Passages*, H.D.'s *Tribute to Freud*, Nathaniel Mackey's ongoing *Song of the Andoumboulou*. Its mode is vast, its traditions are diverse and alive, particularly in those cultures still defined by its form, style, and content. One could further argue that our existence has reached the point where almost all poetry equals elegy: the elegy of our ongoing self-ruin. H.D.: *But we are here today in a city of ruin, a world ruined, it might seem, almost past redemption.* In China it is said that the birth of literature began with a cry of despair, specifically the Southern poet Qu Yuan's 372-line shamanistic lament, *Li Sao: On Encountering Sorrow,* written in the fourth century BC. David Hawkes translates:

> The age is discorded in a tumult of changing:
> How can I tarry much longer among them?
> Orchid and iris have lost all their fragrance;
> Flag and melilotus have changed into straw.

In the fifth century, Liu Xie classified thirty-four different styles of writing in what is considered China's earliest book of literary criticism, *The Literary Mind and the Carving of Dragons.* Three of these styles – *sao* (of *Li Sao*), *lei*, and *ai* – can be considered forms of elegy, though it is also evident that the elegiac permeates so much of classical Chinese poetry through themes of parting, exile, separated lovers, corrupt government, the transience of the red-dust world, the inexorability of passing time, and on and on. In modern times, traditional Chinese poetic styles and structural patterns were largely abandoned in the early twentieth century during the May Fourth Movement, which in the literary sphere embraced open forms and the vernacular. The phrase 挽诗 (*wanshi*), or 挽歌 (*wange*), is generally used to mean elegy, its original signification the poetic inscriptions brushed onto funeral banners. Mining a little deeper into the language this phrase also can be translated as 'pull poetry/song', for 挽 (*wan*) in written records was substituted as a homonym for 輓 (*wan*), which referred to the pallbearers who pulled the imperial funeral cart to the tomb. Mourning song as the creaking axle of the cart. None of the above-noted characters for 'elegy', however, appear in the title of Liu Xiaobo's book, which is called 《念念六四》 *Nian Nian Liu Si* – *Liu Si* being 4/6 (i.e., June Fourth) and *Nian Nian* containing shades of remember/read/study/miss, but the tone and essence evoked is *June Fourth Elegies*.

On 18 March, 1926, during a demonstration that began at Tiananmen against the warlord government and foreign imperialism, the military police opened fire, killing at least forty-seven people and injuring at least two hundred. Lu Xun, arguably the most influential writer of modernist China, wrote an impassioned essay on the same day of the massacre called 'More Roses without Blooms' that was widely quoted after the bloodshed of June Fourth: 'Lies written in ink can never disguise facts written in blood. Blood debts must be repaid in kind. The longer the delay, the greater the interest.' Soon after that he wrote his famous piece 'In Memory of the Noble Miss Liu Hezhen', which Liu Xiaobo quotes in his introduction, and a year later in March 1927 he would write of the victims in his 'Random Notes on the Yellow Flower Festival': 'I am not saying that everyone every day should memorialise the martyrs with tears of bitter sorrow – an annual day of remembrance is enough.' These words could serve as a fitting epigraph to *June Fourth Elegies*, especially in the light of Liu Xiaobo's statement that 'all Lu Xun did provides a starting point for contemporary Chinese intellectuals' own self-reflection'.

Many people in the world first heard of Liu Xiaobo when he won the Nobel Peace Prize on 8 October, 2010. Though he had been a prominent activist and writer in China for over two decades, besides a handful of essays in scholarly journals and anthologies, none of his writing was available in English, and even his dozen or so books in Chinese were either out of print or impossible to find in the US. Due to Liu's dissident blacklist status of twenty-plus years in China, this isn't too surprising; but then it's also true that relatively few writers of modern and contemporary China have been translated and published in this country. Even the bulk of Lu Xun's essays still aren't available, and his stories only in recent months have found their consummate translator in Julia Lovell. China, though, certainly isn't a special case in this regard as historically the US has been broadly aggressive about spreading its own culture and economy to the rest of the world while being indifferent, or averse, to the cultural inflow of other peoples. On the day the Nobel Prize was announced, Liu Xiaobo was in prison and the most widely read response in China was composed by Han Han, the nation's most famous novelist and race-car-driving blogger, who posted this concrete poetic comment: ' '. One can see this as a clever statement about censorship in China, though another translation could be: Let us not forget that Alfred Nobel amassed his fortune from patenting nitroglycerine and dynamite.

Liu Xiaobo was born in the city of Changchun, Jilin province in 1955. In the 1970s he moved with his father to Inner Mongolia and was later sent to the countryside as an educated youth for two years. As Liu told Geremie Barmé – an Australian who was among the first scholars outside of China to write about his work – there he read the only books available to him: the forty-volume complete works of Marx. Liu was part of the sealed-can generation that was raised during the Cultural Revolution. Later in life he would write about this time, 'We grew up in a kind of earthshaking revolutionary slogan, music, and song. In the orthodox communist education we received, we knew nothing but revolution, selfless dedication in the spirit of "fear not hardship, fear not death", the concepts and culture of cold class struggle that lacked any sense of humanity, hatred to others, and the language of violence. We never received an education that was close to life and earthbound, that respected others.' From 1976 until his matriculation at Jilin University in 1977, Liu worked as a wall-painter for the Changchun Construction Company. In 1982, he graduated from Jilin University with a BA in Chinese Literature. He then continued his studies at Beijing Normal University and received a MA and PhD in Literature in 1988. While still a graduate student, Liu burst onto the literary scene with a scathing critique of post-Cultural Revolution literature called 'Crisis! The Literature of the New Age Is Facing Crisis'. In coarse language and with a pronounced stutter, he presented his essay at a conference for the Literature Research Institute at the Chinese Academy of Social Sciences. It was then promptly published in the *Shenzen Youth Daily*, and epithets describing him as a 'black horse' and 'cultural nihilist' appeared in the Chinese press.

A year later, in 1987, Liu published his critique *A Dialogue with Li Zehou*, which he later revised and published as *A Critique of Choice* in Taiwan in 1989. Li Zehou was one of the most revered thinkers in China during the 'culture fever' of the 1980s. An establishment intellectual who wrote about Chinese aesthetics ('the art of living') through the lens of Western philosophy, particularly Kant, Li's books were eventually banned by the government after Tiananmen, and he moved to the U.S. where he has lived ever since. Kent M. Peterson who translated the *Dialogue* for an issue of *Chinese Studies in Philosophy* used four adjectives to describe Liu Xiaobo's prose: 'meandering, verbose, difficult, and interesting'. At the time, Liu was deeply influenced by the writings of Rousseau and Nietzsche, and he begins his *Dialogue* with a professed admiration of Li Zehou's writings before going on to subvert and negate the gists and piths of Li's thought. At one point Liu traces Li Zehou's 'bad habit of self-beautification' to Qu Yuan's *Li Sao*, which Liu describes as a 'highly rationalised and moralised beggarly plea of indignation.' This is a sweeping bit of polemic typical of Liu Xiaobo's biting *zawen*-style prose, a style popularised by Lu Xun that careens along rhetorical extremes to strengthen its arguments. Readers of Chinese literature know that the *Li Sao* is a poem as cherished as *The Iliad*, commentated on through the centuries by a host of luminaries, 'a great classic of poetic metaphor and allegory,' the scholar Qian Zhongshu writes, 'written in expansive and unbounded language. It contains many lines that are unconstrained by reality, just as it has lines that will not stand up to verification by experience.' Liu's comparison can be interpreted as a bit of subversion that serves to heighten the satiric tone underlying his position, though at times such stylistic operations in trying to reveal a grain of truth risk gross generalisations. He goes on to write in the *Dialogue*, 'Only Ji Kang [a third century philosopher], Li Bo [the great Tang poet], Li Zhi [an anti-Confucianist Ming Dynasty philosopher], and a handful of other geniuses who despised tradition, ridiculed the nobility, mocked the sage, revolted against reality, and sought individual freedom after the manner of Lao Zi and Zhuang Zi, at the same time endowing this freedom with a passionate content that was worldly, sensate, and instinctual.' For the Liu Xiaobo of the *Dialogue*, 'Confucius is dead. Li Zehou is old. Traditional Chinese culture ought to have had its last successor long ago.' Liu defines this traditional culture as a Rousseauian return to antiquity, an ideal that Chinese intellectuals have returned to in comfort and safety because of 'the shattering of Enlightenment ideals'.

While a lecturer at Beijing Normal University in 1988, Liu Xiaobo's doctoral thesis was published as *Aesthetics and Human Freedom* and later published in Taiwan as *Tragedy, Aesthetics, Freedom*. From 1988 until his return to Beijing in April 1989 to join the June Fourth Movement, Liu was a visiting scholar at the University of Oslo, University of Hawaii, and Columbia University, while writing prodigiously for various newspapers in Hong Kong. His time abroad was an eye-opening experience. In May 1989 he wrote, 'When New York tore away all of the external embellishments and illusory fame that I had in China, I suddenly realised how weak I really was. . . . All I could do was "ingratiate myself" with Western culture – glorifying it in a manner quite out of proportion to reality, as if it not only held the key to China's salvation, but contained all the answers to the world's problems.' And in another essay about his time abroad: 'I frequently heard praise such as "It's the first time I've ever heard a Chinese speak like that" or "That a Chinese can have such an understanding of Western philosophy!" or again, "How could China have produced such a rebel like yourself?". . . . Every time I heard this kind of approbation I felt like I hadn't left China, but rather had been stuffed into somebody else's luggage and thrown onto a plane as a curiosity item to be taken to a strange land. Where they decide to place you is where you have to be.' The last two books Liu Xiaobo published openly in China appeared in 1989: *The Fog of Metaphysics* and *Walking Naked toward God*.

June Fourth became the transformative fire in Liu's life that politicised him as a non-violent activist around issues of free speech and human rights. Geremie Barmé in his essay 'Confession, Redemption, and Death: Liu Xiaobo and the Protest Movement of 1989' documents some of Liu Xiaobo's activities during Tiananmen, pointing out that only a few years earlier Liu was critical and dismissive of the 1986 student demonstrations. But whatever reservations he originally might have had about the protest quickly expanding around the Monument to the People's Heroes that April must have been slight compared with the fervour in which he returned. Liu's protest activities included drafting questionnaires to assess public opinion about the demonstrations, writing appeals to overseas Chinese and foreigners for donations to support the cause, as well as spending many days demonstrating with the students and workers on the Square – and all the logistics of food, drink, shelter that entailed. A few days after martial law was announced on 23 May, the Independent Student Union of Beijing Normal University published Liu's 'Six-Point Program for Democracy' as 'Our Suggestions', which called for the end of martial law and student solidarity with workers and peasants in a rational, non-violent process of democratic change through 'the growth of civic consciousness'. On 2 June Liu along with three others – Zhou Duo, Jou Dejian, and Gao Xin – began what would be the last hunger strike of the Movement with the publication of their 'Hunger Strike Declaration'. This manifesto not only emphasised the students' 'legal, non-violent, rational, and peaceful means to fight for freedom, democracy, and human rights', but also recognised the limitations of the student movement, its 'disorderly internal organisation' and 'excessive sense of privilege but inadequate sense of equality,' while calling on all sympathisers and supporters to be 'participators in the building up of democracy'. It also called on the government to acknowledge its own mistakes so that these could be 'turned into a positive asset as a means to learn to govern our country democratically'. The declaration outlined four main watchwords: '1) We have no enemies! Don't poison our consciousness and the democratisation of China with hatred and violence. 2) We all need introspection! Everyone is responsible for China's backwardness. 3) We are first and foremost citizens! 4) We are not in search of death – we are looking for real life.' As military troops and tanks entered the Square in the early hours of 4 June, Liu gave a speech asking the students to disperse in order to avoid bloodshed. At some point in the ensuing chaos, he lost his passport and identity card on the Square.

On June 6 Liu Xiaobo was arrested and imprisoned for twenty months. He was fired from his teaching post, his books were banned, papers confiscated, and since then he has been prohibited from both public employment and from publishing in China. But while Liu was in prison two books of his were published in Taiwan: *Mysteries of Thought and Dreams of Mankind*, a two-volume edition culled from his previous books, and *Contemporary Chinese Politics and Intellectuals*, which was first serialised in the Hong Kong newspaper *Cheng Ming* and has been reissued again in Taiwan in 2010. Meanwhile, the Youth Press of China printed a collection of his works called *Liu Xiaobo: The Man and his Machinations* to add to the denunciations all over the news. The novelist Ma Jian, however, wrote an encomium for his monthly publication titled 'Liu Xiaobo: The Bravest Man of his Generation'. Liu wasn't so ebullient about himself. His *Monologue of a Doomsday Survivor* published in Taiwan in 1992 is a confession of the confession he had been coerced to make in order to be released from prison. Liu's statement was broadcast on television and has continued to haunt him ever since, as is evident in his introduction to the *Elegies*. In the *Monologue* he also continued to critique the June Fourth Movement, a theme he picks up in his impassioned essay 'That Holy Word "Revolution"' written in 1994 for *Popular Protest and Political Culture in Modern China*, edited by Jeffrey N. Wasserstrom and Elizabeth J. Perry. In retrospect, Liu argues, Tiananmen was one revolution in a history of 'heavenly mandated' revolutions in China that had actually interrupted and delayed the Communist Party's democratisation process. In the revolutionary climate of 1989, students and intellectuals had become 'extremely conceited – just as if we had reverted to the time of the Cultural Revolution and felt ourselves to be the most revolutionary', and 'the democracy we sought during the movement was too empty, too emotional, and did not go beyond the exciting, romantic stage of hollow slogans and idealism of our newly formed consciousness'. Furthermore, in the aftermath of Tiananmen, Liu felt that the more open, relaxed atmosphere earlier in the decade had been replaced by 'an atmosphere of antagonism, tension, and terror'. He argued that the cooperation of popular opposition groups should allow the gradual self-reform of the Communist Party, which above all must involve the Party taking responsibility for their own criminal actions during June Fourth: 'All that needs to be done is to privately compensate the kin of the June Fourth victims; release all June Fourth political prisoners; restore to their former positions those who, because of June Fourth, were unfairly treated; gradually remove and demote those who rose to power on the blood of June Fourth; and allow those who fled overseas because of June Fourth to safely return.' From the start such tasks require a public confession of guilt the authorities have yet to make.

During the months that followed the Tiananmen tragedy, it is difficult to imagine the degree of darkness and despair that spread across the country. The poet Duo Duo had witnessed students cutting themselves with glass as the troops moved into the Square, and in the days and months that unfolded many poets and writers didn't choose the path of indifference and self-intoxication, nor the path of withdrawing from the world with a knowing smile, but chose, like Qu Yuan, the path of suicide. A month before the national crisis drove students all over the country to demonstrate, the renowned poet Haizi killed himself near Shanhai Pass by lying down on some railroad tracks. The young poet Xi Chuan, who recently edited Haizi's *Complete Poems* in China, called Haizi's death 'their generation's first myth'. The exiled poet Gu Cheng, while living in Berlin in 1992, wrote in the preface to his last poem cycle 'City: June Fourth': *I am a dead man, alive in a dying moment.* Less than a year later Gu Cheng would kill himself and his wife on the idyllic Waiheke Island. Scholar and literary critic Wang Yuechuan describes the hopeless post-Tiananmen void in 'A Perspective on the Suicide of Chinese

Poets in the 1990s': 'When a dozen minor poets died in various parts of China, I was surprised to discover that people were no longer interested even in the suicide of poets; poetry is no longer read nor is the death of poets the concern of the public. Poets have become useless beings and poetry has become useless goods. Or it may be said that when poetry has lost the ability to speak the truth, the poet commits suicide and so does poetry.'

Liu was released from prison in January 1991. From January to May of 1993 he travelled to Australia and the US to be interviewed for the documentary film *The Gate of Heavenly Peace*. In May 1995 Liu was placed under house arrest for releasing a petition that demanded government reparations for the Tiananmen Massacre. He was released in January 1996, and a month later married his second wife, Liu Xia, a poet and artist who has been the one sustaining presence in Liu Xiaobo's life, and who, in her own words, has lived periods of 'intense loneliness and desperation as a convict's wife'. In October of that year, Liu Xiaobo co-authored the October Tenth Declaration with Wang Xizhe, which among other things upheld the peaceful reunification of Taiwan and China, acknowledged the rights of the Tibetan people to self-determination as Sun Yat-sen had proclaimed over seventy years before in his First Congress to the Guomindang, and called for the impeachment of then General Secretary Jiang Zemin for stating that the national military is 'under the Communist Party's absolute leadership' and not under the Central Military Commission as it is written in the Constitution. For this he was sentenced to three years in a manual labour re-education camp in Dalian.

Upon his release in October 1999, Liu continued to write, mainly publishing his articles in Hong Kong and eventually on the internet. More books followed: in 2000 a collection of literary criticism, *A Beauty Gave Me a Knockout Drug*, co-authored with Wang Shuo under the pen name Lao Xia was published on the Mainland; his first collection of poems *The Selected Poems of Liu Xiaobo and Liu Xia*, a correspondence through poetry written during his incarceration, was published in Hong Kong with a preface by Liao Yiwu; in 2002, *Facing a Nation That Lies to Its Conscience* appeared in Taiwan; and in

2005 and 2006, *Civil Awakening* and *A Single Blade and Toxic Sword: Critique of Chinese Nationalism* were published in Chinese in the US. Awards and recognition also followed: from 2003 to 2007 Liu served as the President of the Independent Chinese PEN Centre and in 2004 he received the Fondation de France Prize from Reporters Without Borders and the Annual Human Rights Press Award in Hong Kong. That same year, Liu Xia once said in an interview, the Ministry of Public Security searched their home and confiscated most of Liu Xiaobo's unpublished writings.

In December 2008, Liu Xiaobo with other draftees released Charter 08, an anti-authoritarian pro-democracy manifesto that echoed the initiatives of the Czechoslovakian civil rights appeal, Charter 77. Liu was detained and not formally arrested until June 23, 2009, and held without trial until 23 December, 2009, when he was sentenced to eleven years in prison for 'counter-revolutionary propaganda and incitement to crime' and 'inciting subversion of state power'. At his trial he made a final statement that directly echoed the 'Hunger Strike Declaration' he co-authored twenty years earlier during Tiananmen: 'I have no enemies and no hatred. None of the police who monitored, arrested, and interrogated me, none of the prosecutors who indicted me, and none of the judges who judged me are my enemies.' Earlier in 2009 he had published another book in Taiwan, *A Superpower Sinks: A Memo to China.* He had also received the PEN/ Barbara Goldsmith Freedom to Write Award, and as neither he nor his wife could be present to accept the award in New York, Liu Xia sent some words to be read at the ceremony. A passage from the transcript translated by Liao Tienchi reads:

> I have not come to view Xiaobo as a political figure. In my eyes, he has always been and will always be an awkward and diligent poet. Even in prison, he has continued to write his poems. When the warden took away his paper and pen, he simply pulled his verse out of thin air. Over the past twenty years, Xiaobo and I have accumulated hundreds of such poems, which were born of the conversations between our souls.

I feel that Xiaobo is using his intensity and passion as a poet to push the democracy movement forward in China. He shouts passionately as a poet 'no, no, no' to the dictators.

In private, he whispers gently to the dead souls of June Fourth, who, to this day, have not received justice, as well as to me and to all his dear friends: 'yes, yes'.

•

I've pieced together this brief background of Liu Xiaobo's thought and lifework with the distressing sense that such a bio-panoptic view not only leaves out so much of the life being sketched, but also leaves out so many others who in the spirit of the June Fourth Movement have been working steadily for social reform in China along with Liu. But outlining the barest of context, if only to let the poems in this collection radiate beyond the boundaries of context, does remind me that poetry and literature cannot come into existence without the life that makes it. No matter how imaginative or fantastic the work is it constantly lures us into the real that is always much more than simple biography. How can we read Kafka, for one among infinite instances, without being drawn toward (or repelled by) the Worker's Accident Insurance Institute? Or listen to Mandelstam's music without conjuring the shadow of the Stalinist state? And what of *June Fourth Elegies*?

I first read Liu Xiaobo's poems in the summer of 2009 when David Haglund, the managing editor of the literary journal *PEN America*, emailed me some of Liu's poems and asked if I'd want to translate a few for their next issue. At the time I only knew Liu Xiaobo through his activism during June Fourth and had no idea he was a poet. I tried my hand at translating four of the poems, which ended up being published in *PEN America 11: Make Believe*. To further disbelief, some of these poems were read publicly by Paul Auster, and a couple months later by Edward Albee, Don DeLillo, and E. L. Doctorow on the steps of the New York Public Library during a protest of Liu Xiaobo's imprisonment. The *Guardian* covered this demonstration in an article published 4 January, 2010. A fifth poem, 'Greed's Prisoner', I translated at the request of Larry Siems, the director of PEN America's Freedom to Write Program, which was later read by Victoria Redel at the PEN World Voices Festival Gala in April 2010. Since then, it has been remarkable to see these poems reappear in magazines and newspapers around the world, one even translated from the English into Danish and printed as a broadsheet in the newspaper *Politiken* on the day of the Nobel ceremony. Much later I also discovered that these five poems all originally appeared in Liu Xiaobo and Liu Xia's volume of correspondence poems. I've included them in the last section of this book titled 'Five Poems for Liu Xia'.

In the summer of 2010 Larry Siems visited Liu Xia in Beijing. She gave him two books that he eventually passed on to me: a copy of the *Selected Poems* and a copy of *June Fourth Elegies*. Unlike the former edition no publication information appeared inside the *Elegies*. It opened with a dedication to the activist group the Tiananmen Mothers and *to those who can remember*. A photographic spread of Liu Xiaobo and other demonstrators during June Fourth followed, and then on the next page, right before the introduction Liu had originally written as an elegy for the year 2000, a spare one-page biographical chronology appeared, the last entry of which stated that the book was published sometime after the release of Charter 08 while Liu was under house arrest in an undisclosed location in Beijing. The whole of the edition was threaded together with images of Liu Xia's art: the first half interspersed with otherworldly black-and-white photographs of dolls with stunned expressions staged in various terrifying scenes – one bound with rope before an open book, another impaled by wooden stakes; the second half interspersed with paintings in muted colours of trees, tracks, drips, ghostly figures. It was a mysterious book, and the poems burned with a gritty emotional intensity intensified by the fact that Liu was once again in prison for voicing beliefs contrary to the state. What I found most moving about the collection, however, was the ritualistic structure of the whole that spanned twenty years of elegising the same historic event, year after year. One might see it as an act of madness, or futility. For me it expressed a profound act of remembrance, an affirmative force of belief over a sorrow-filled image corrupted by time, indifference, and forgetting.

A friend of Liu Xia's told me that around five hundred copies of the *Elegies* were privately printed in Hong Kong as gifts to be given away to friends and family. She said one of Liu Xiaobo's friends tried to bring some copies to the Mainland, but that the person was detained and the books confiscated. A few others who were familiar with Liu's essays told me that they didn't even know he wrote poetry until his *Selected Poems* appeared in 2000. On the internet I found a photograph of Liu posing with friends in a field during his undergraduate years with a caption saying they were part of a poetry group called Chizi Xin (Red-Bared Hearts). Perhaps a mix of the neo-romantic with youthful camaraderie, the group has evidently left no Acmeist or *menglong* Misty Poet traces. One significant thing to note is that the only two poetry books Liu Xiaobo has published have been written from a place of oppressive darkness – his first collection written while he was in prison, and essentially a collection of love poems between husband and wife who are unjustly separated by an authoritarian state; his second poetry book annual elegies for a nationwide tragedy caused and silenced by the state, a tragedy the poet is a victim of and witnessed directly, a tragedy the poet has continued to suffer directly through harassment, total censorship, exclusion from public employment, and imprisonment. The American writer Fanny Howe describes the poems of Holocaust survivor Ilona Karmel in a similar vein: 'The very fact that she wrote poetry in Buchenwald suggests that poetry itself is a part of the mind reserved for resistance to force. Poetry doesn't just help someone survive, it is a survivor itself: fluid, protean, as it passes through walls, and brings a particular beat to a way of thinking and being.' If the beat in Liu's poetry can be described as political, it is so in the sense of being engaged with the times, engaged with the real of society happening around him, as a way to resist the suffocating darkness. There is no propaganda, no sloganeering, no browbeating political agenda in the *Elegies*. Even the word 'democracy' is only used twice in the poems, once in reference to democracy activists' beer glasses, and once as a proper noun to refer to the Goddess of Democracy statue that was raised in the Square during June Fourth – the Goddess who gazed directly into the eyes of Mao's portrait hanging on the Gate of Heavenly Peace. A more literal translation of the statue would be 'Goddess of Liberty' but it is widely known by the former name, and its intended model wasn't the Statue of Liberty but the Russian sculptor Vera Mukhina's stainless steel *A Worker and Collective Farm Woman* that graced the Soviet Pavilion at the 1937 Paris World's Fair.

The translator dreams of exact equivalences. If translation is one language mourning its limitations, in the same cry the other language celebrates anew. The one and the other continuously switch roles during this process while the translator hardly knows what's happening between words. Liu has distilled his complex, meandering prose sentences into not always concise poetic lines that rarely enjamb to disperse meaning but do run over the ends of lines to the next in a kind of conversational free verse. Each line usually functions as a parsed phrase within a sentence though this is complicated by the absence of any punctuation and by certain lines that hinge between the line above and the line below – a syntactical flexibility that seems especially inbred in the Chinese language itself. There are also places in the poems where unrhymed couplets form a structural parallelism, or lines are dictated by a repeated grammatical structure that give each line the same number of characters. I decided to use capitalisation to suggest the start of a new sentence or thought, and kept the absence of punctuation to allow meaning to run across lines, particularly where a hinging effect in the original occurs. For the *Elegies*, I have also followed the same number of lines per poem in the translation as in the Chinese.

Earlier, I quoted Liu Xia's description of her husband as an 'awkward and diligent poet'. Though this comes across as somewhat endearing, I feel it's also an honest observation of Liu Xiaobo's poetry. Liu isn't a wildly imaginative innovator like Gu Cheng (who was born the year after Liu) nor is he as linguistically nuanced or disciplined as, say, Celan in 'Death Fugue', where the music's technical brilliance coincides so perfectly with its horrifying imagery to form a prayer one has never heard before (though the *Elegies*, too, are written from the perspective of the dead and forgotten). Liu prefers a bold, in-your-face directness in his poetry, and veers away from abstractions and elusiveness. Whole lines in a later elegy are even repeated verbatim from an elegy written years earlier. This fatigue, however, can be said to mirror the static sameness of blank memory – year after year of perseverance in the face of hopelessness and an unchanging political landscape that has mostly changed by becoming more materialistic and corrupt. Liu's morally serious and impassioned tone is also balanced (or offset?) by a severe streak of black humour that feeds off the irony of the times, sucking it dry. His lyrical, antinomian lines scathe deep into his government's crimes.

Several recurring images appear throughout the elegies. Blood and its compound meanings are prevalent in connection to the disaster and memory of June Fourth, and also resonates as a frequently invoked actualised symbol in Chinese poetry, especially during its modern revolutionary history from the late Qing, as with the poet Tan Sitong, through the May Fourth Crescent Moon Society poets and on through the twentieth century. Tiananmen Square itself also figures large in the *Elegies*. As *the* national symbol of China that the government has tried and failed to depoliticise over the years, it had been the site of numerous mass demonstrations long before June Fourth and has become, as Liu writes in his third anniversary offering, *a justified absolute / that suffocates all life*. The art historian Wu Hung has written a remarkable book about the Square, *Remaking Beijing*, that delves into its five hundred year history, from its original design as a map of heaven, an image of *Yi Jing* hexagrams, its site of imperial 'cloud tray' ceremonies and, during the Ming dynasty, biannual death sentence trials, to its modern period of destruction, renovation, and concrete expansion. As Wu Hung notes, the space of Tiananmen Square since 1977 has been defined by five monuments, which form a distinct axis between official past and present. There is the northern point, Tiananmen, the ancient Gate of Heavenly Peace, from which Mao announced the birth of the People's Republic. In the west stands the Great Hall of the People and in the east the Museum of Chinese History, both constructed during Mao's rule. To the south is the Chairman Mao Memorial Hall (or Mausoleum) erected on the anniversary of Mao's death, and in the centre of the Square 'like a needle on an enormous sundial' stands Mao's Monument to the People's Heroes, completed in 1958. In the longest chapter of his book, Wu Hung turns to avant-garde artists whose work has formed a kind of 'anti-monument' that challenges the state's repression of Tiananmen's history by creating 'a space for individual remembrance and imagination'. Liu Xiaobo's *Elegies* is certainly part of this socio-cultural tradition of space-creating memory.

One recurring noun in *June Fourth Elegies* I'd like to mention because of its central importance in Liu's book is 亡灵, *wangling*. The primary meaning of *wang* is 'to flee', with other meanings of 'be lost', 'die or perish', 'dead', or 'fall or subjugate'; *ling* in ancient times referred to a certain type of female shaman, though now in different contexts can mean anything from 'quick and clever' to 'mind, soul, spirit, intelligence', to 'efficacious', to 'a coffin, or remains of the deceased'. *Wang* is also a homonym for another *wang* that means 'to forget'. Together the two characters make a noun, *wangling*, that refers to the soul of the deceased, the spirit that lives on after death, a ghost or spectre. As the phrase appears so many times throughout the book, I've translated it three different ways depending on rhythm and context in order to suggest the various resonances in the Chinese: 'dead soul', 'departed spirit', and 'departed soul'. Some dark voice wants me to translate it as *duende*, 'the same duende that scorched the heart of Nietzsche' as Lorca writes – the poem that must be possessed by duende, that 'makes us suffer by means of a drama of living forms', that sees death's approach: 'When the angel sees death come, he flies in slow circles and weaves tears of narcissus and ice into elegy we have seen trembling in the hands of Keats, Villasandino, Herrera, Bécquer, and Juan Ramón Jiménez'. While this would be an obvious gaffe in the context of this translation – as the two words are far from cultural cognates – the barest shades of *wangling* and *duende* do converge in 'soul' as living spirit-force, reaching back into the mythic origins of their respective languages.

The most painful thing about translating this collection was not being able to consult with Liu Xiaobo or Liu Xia – the former serving his eleven-year prison sentence, the latter under strict house arrest. It was an unnerving, unsettling experience to think of Liu Xiaobo's isolation while fiddling with his ruptured lines from the tomb. My study is a room with open doors and windows; my country a democracy of drone planes killing Pakistani and Afghani villagers, a democracy of more prisoners than any other nation, of *privatised* prisons, people directly used for private and public profit. And there the walls of Angel Island, there Guantanamo. China, meanwhile, holds around a trillion dollars in US bonds. Or elsewhere consider the artist Owen Maseko who was recently arrested in Bulawayo, Zimbabwe, for organising an art exhibition around the memory of the Gukurahundi Massacre. Or the circle of Tahrir Square and the Arab Spring. Where does the code of signals lead to and through? Toward what reckonings and reconciliations? There is no ground here for self-righteousness to root. The only conversation I could have with Liu was through his poems, through the verb of translation, thinking of what I thought he might say to a certain translation choice along the way. Trying to hear the happening in his words, here in the persona of a wooden plank:

> let me simply move-
> not-move, ever so tightly nestle in
> together crushed by steel into dust
> that falls into the fissures of asphalt
> in Beijing at the entrance to the Six Ministries
> into the soil beds along Chang'an Avenue
> transforms into perennial-spring ivy
> preserver of memory

In the silence of this conversation I was reminded of two conceptions of freedom at play as it translates into today's everyday. Orlando Patterson has lucidly argued that our idea of freedom is a socially constructed value that arose from the necessary consequence of resisting and negating slavery – that 'without slavery there would have been no freedmen'. One can even see that the concept of 'freedom' in Chinese, 自由 (*ziyou*), entered the language via Japanese translations of Western texts. For Octavio Paz, 'the end of artistic activity is not the finished work but freedom. The work is the road and nothing more. This freedom is ambiguous or, rather, it is conditional: we can lose it at any moment, above all if we take ourselves or our work too seriously.' The former idea leads into society, the latter idea leads back to the individual and Zhuang Zi's 'revolt against reality' as Liu Xiaobo puts it. The two converge at a third and fourth conception. Interrogating and negotiating these means and ends is a way to turn straw back into flag and melilotus, transmute honey into sun, transform dust into perennial-spring ivy. It is also the work of elegy, translation, and poetry.

•

I am grateful to David Haglund and Larry Siems at the PEN American Center for first introducing me to Liu Xiaobo's poetry and for trusting me to translate his work despite my initial reservations. Thanks to Liu Xiaobo's agent Peter Bernstein, to Tienchi Martin-Liao for sharing her thoughts about Liu Xiaobo's work, and to three of Liu Xia's friends for information about the original publication of *June Fourth Elegies*. Thanks also to the Lannan Foundation for providing the time and space for me to complete a draft of this translation, and to Fiona McCrae, Katie Dublinski, Erin Kottke, my tireless editor Jeffrey Shotts, and the rest of the staff at Graywolf Press for their support, and encouragement. The circle of thanks continues to Robin Robertson at Jonathan Cape for bringing this book to further shores. And a deep note of gratitude to Andrea Lingenfelter for her helpful feedback on the proofs. This translation is dedicated to Liu Xiaobo and Liu Xia:

雌 雄 終 不 隔
神 物 會 當 逢
(李白)

JEFFREY YANG
June 2011